Finance and Economics Discussion Series
Divisions of Research & Statistics and Monetary Affairs
Federal Reserve Board, Washington, D.C.

Monetary Policy Alternatives at the Zero Bound:
An Empirical Assessment

Ben S. Bernanke, Vincent R. Reinhart, and Brian P. Sack

2004-48

Monetary Policy Alternatives at the Zero Bound: An Empirical Assessment

Ben S. Bernanke[*]
Board of Governors of the Federal Reserve System

Vincent R. Reinhart
Board of Governors of the Federal Reserve System

Brian P. Sack
Macroeconomic Advisers

ABSTRACT

The success over the years in reducing inflation and, consequently, the average level of nominal interest rates has increased the likelihood that the nominal policy interest rate may become constrained by the zero lower bound. When that happens, a central bank can no longer stimulate aggregate demand by further interest-rate reductions and must rely on "non-standard" policy alternatives. To assess the potential effectiveness of such policies, we analyze the behavior of selected asset prices over short periods surrounding central bank statements or other types of financial or economic news and estimate "no-arbitrage" models of the term structure for the United States and Japan. There is some evidence that central bank communications can help to shape public expectations of future policy actions and that asset purchases in large volume by a central bank would be able to affect the price or yield of the targeted asset.

JEL CLASSIFICATION: E41, E42, E58, E61
KEYWORDS: Deflation, zero bound, monetary policy, term structure, policy expectations

---

[*] The views expressed are our own and are not necessarily shared by anyone else in the Federal Reserve System. We have benefited from conversations with many colleagues. This paper was presented to the Brookings Panel on Economic Activity, September 9, 2004. We also thank Thomas Gallagher of the ISI Group and Jeffrey Young of Nikko/Citigroup for providing data on their real-time interpretations of, respectively, U.S. and Japanese monetary policies.

Non-technical summary

Central banks usually implement monetary policy by setting the short-term nominal interest rate, such as the federal funds rate in the United States. However, the success over the years in reducing inflation and, consequently, the average level of nominal interest rates has increased the likelihood that the nominal policy interest rate may become constrained by the zero lower bound on interest rates. When that happens, a central bank can no longer stimulate aggregate demand by further interest-rate reductions and must rely instead on "non-standard" policy alternatives.

An extensive literature has discussed monetary policy alternatives at the zero bound, but for the most part from a theoretical or historical perspective. Few studies have presented empirical evidence on the potential effectiveness of non-standard monetary policies in modern economies. Such evidence obviously would help central banks plan for the contingency of the policy rate at zero and also bear directly on the choice of the appropriate inflation objective in normal times: The greater the confidence of central bankers that tools exist to help the economy escape the zero bound, the less need there is to maintain an inflation "buffer," bolstering the argument for a lower inflation objective.

In this paper, we apply the tools of modern empirical finance to the recent experiences of the United States and Japan to provide evidence on the potential effectiveness of various nonstandard policies. Following Bernanke and Reinhart (2004), we group these policy alternatives into three classes: (1) using communications policies to shape public expectations about the future course of interest rates; (2) increasing the size of the central bank's balance sheet, or "quantitative easing"; and (3) changing the composition of the central bank's balance sheet through, for example, the targeted purchases of long-term bonds as a means of reducing the long-term interest rate. We describe how these policies might work and discuss relevant existing evidence.

To garner new evidence concerning nonstandard policy options, we employ two approaches. First, we measure and analyze the behavior of selected asset prices and yields over short periods surrounding central bank statements or other types of financial or economic news (an "event-study" analysis). Second, we estimate "no-arbitrage" models of the term structure for the United States and Japan. For any given set of macroeconomic conditions and stance of monetary policy, these models allow us to predict interest rates at all maturities. Using the predicted term structure as a benchmark, we are then able to assess whether factors not included in the model—such as the Bank of Japan's quantitative easing policy—have economically significant effects on rates.

Our results provide some grounds for optimism about the likely efficacy of nonstandard policies. In particular, we confirm a potentially important role for central bank communications to try to shape public expectations of future policy actions. Like Gürkaynak, Sack, and Swanson (2004), we find that the Federal Reserve's monetary policy decisions have two distinct effects on asset prices. These factors represent, respectively, (1) the unexpected change in the current setting of the federal funds rate, and (2) the change in market expectations about the trajectory of the funds rate over the next year that is not explained by the current policy action. In the United States, the second factor, in particular, appears strongly linked to Fed policy statements, probably reflecting the importance of communication by the central bank. If central bank "talk" affects policy expectations, then policymakers retain some leverage over long-term yields, even if the current policy rate is at or near zero.

We also find evidence supporting the view that asset purchases in large volume by a central bank would be able to affect the price or yield of the targeted asset. Since the Federal Reserve has not engaged in such purchases in the past fifty years, our evidence for the United States is necessarily indirect. Three recent episodes, however, provide important insights. In each, financial market participants received information that led them to expect large changes in the relative supplies of Treasury securities. These episodes include (1) the Treasury's announcements of "debt buybacks" that followed the emergence of budget surpluses in the late 1990s; (2) the massive foreign official purchases of U.S. Treasury securities over the past two years; and (3) the apparent belief among market participants in 2003 that the Federal Reserve was actively considering targeted purchases of Treasury securities as an anti-deflationary measure. Event-study analyses of these episodes, as well as the comparison of actual Treasury yields during these periods to our estimated benchmark for the term structure, suggest that large changes in the relative supplies of securities may have economically significant effects on their yields.

Our analysis of the recent experience in Japan focuses on two non-standard policies recently employed by the Bank of Japan (BOJ): (1) the zero-interest-rate policy (ZIRP), under which the BOJ committed to keep the call rate at zero until deflation has been eliminated; and (2) the BOJ's quantitative easing policy, which consists of providing bank reserves at levels much greater than needed to maintain a policy rate of zero. Our evidence for the effectiveness of these policies is more mixed than in the case of the United States. The event-study analyses, which may be less informative in Japan because of small sample sizes, do not provide clear conclusions. We then employ our estimated term-structure model for Japan to account for the effects of the zero lower bound on policy expectations and hence longer-dated yields. Simulations of the model indicate that interest rates at all maturities were noticeably lower under both non-standard policies than they would have been otherwise.

Despite our relatively encouraging findings concerning the potential efficacy of non-standard policies at the zero bound, caution remains appropriate in making policy prescriptions. Although it appears that non-standard policy measures may affect asset prices and yields and, consequently, aggregate demand, considerable uncertainty remains about the size and reliability of these effects under the circumstances prevailing near the zero bound. The conservative approach—maintaining a sufficient inflation buffer and applying preemptive easing as necessary to minimize the risk of hitting the zero bound— still seems to us to be sensible. However, such policies cannot ensure that the zero bound will never be met, so that additional refining of our understanding of the potential usefulness of nonstandard policies for escaping the zero bound should remain a high priority for macroeconomists.

Monetary Policy Alternatives at the Zero Bound: An Empirical Assessment

The conventional instrument of monetary policy in most major industrial economies is the very short-term nominal interest rate, such as the overnight federal funds rate in the case of the United States. The use of this instrument, however, implies a potential problem: Because currency (which pays a nominal interest rate of zero) can be used as a store of value, the short-term nominal interest rate cannot be pushed below zero. Should the nominal rate hit zero, the real short-term interest rate—at that point equal to the negative of prevailing inflation expectations—may be higher than the rate needed to ensure stable prices and the full utilization of resources. Indeed, there is a possibility of an unstable dynamic, if the excessively high real rate leads to downward pressure on costs and prices that, in turn, raise the real short-term interest rate, which depresses activity and prices further, and so on.

With Japan having suffered from the problems created by the zero lower bound (ZLB) on the nominal interest rate in recent years and with rates in countries such as the United States and Switzerland having also come uncomfortably close, the problems of conducting monetary policy when interest rates approach zero have elicited considerable attention from the economics profession. Some contributions have framed the problem in a formal general equilibrium setting, including, for example, Woodford (2003), Eggertsson and Woodford (2003a,b), Benhabib, Schmitt-Grohé, and Uribe (2003), and Auerbach and Obstfeld (2004). Another strand of the literature has listed and discussed the potential policy options available to central banks when the zero bound is binding; see, for example, Blinder (2000), Bernanke (2002), Clouse et al. (2004), and Bernanke and Reinhart (2004).

Our results provide some grounds for optimism about the likely efficacy of nonstandard policies. In particular, we confirm a potentially important role for central bank communications to shape public expectations of future policy actions, the first type of nonstandard policy. Specifically, our event studies for the United States confirm the result of Gürkaynak, Sack, and Swanson (2004) that surprises in the setting of the current policy rate are not sufficient to explain the effect of monetary policy decisions on policy expectations and asset prices. These effects, however, can be explained by the addition of a second factor that reflects revisions to private-sector expectations about the course of the policy rate over the subsequent year. Changes in the second factor appear strongly linked to Federal Reserve policy statements, providing support to the view that a central bank can help to shape market expectations.

The U.S. record also provides encouraging evidence that changes in the relative supplies of securities significantly affects their relative returns. If it is the case that assets are imperfect substitutes for each other, then changes in the composition of the central bank's balance sheet might be an effective non-standard policy. Many theoretical considerations, however, suggest that the degree of imperfect substitutability among assets should be small. To assess this prediction, we apply the event study methodology to three important episodes in which U.S. financial market participants received information that led them to expect large changes in the relative supplies of Treasury securities: the announcement of "debt buybacks" that followed the emergence of budget surpluses in the late 1990s, the massive foreign official purchases of U.S. Treasury securities over the past two years, and the apparent expectation among market participants in 2003 that the Federal Reserve was likely to embark on targeted bond purchases. The event-study evidence is supplemented by the use of our estimated term structure model, which provides a benchmark against which to compare the actual behavior of Treasury yields during the above three episodes. Our evidence generally supports the view that financial assets are not perfect substitutes, implying that relative supplies do matter for asset pricing.

Our analysis of the recent Japanese experience focuses on two non-standard policies recently employed by the Bank of Japan (BOJ): (1) the zero-interest-rate policy (ZIRP), under which the BOJ has committed to keep the call rate at zero until deflation has been eliminated; and (2) the BOJ's quantitative easing policy, which consists of providing bank reserves at levels much greater than needed to maintain a policy rate of zero. Our evidence for the effectiveness of these policies is more mixed than in the case of the United States. In event-study analyses, which may be less informative in Japan because of small sample sizes, we find no reliable relationship over the past few years between the second factor (one-year-ahead policy expectations) and policy statements by the Bank of Japan. This result, taken on its own, suggests that the Bank of Japan was either unwilling or unable to influence year-ahead expectations during the period considered (though see below).

On a more positive note, Japan provides us the only evidence of recent vintage bearing on the second type of nonstandard policy, changing the size of the central bank's balance sheet (or "quantitative easing"). While this strategy has been used recently in Japan, many consider the manner to which it has been employed to have been relatively restrained and limited. Moreover, other forces have no doubt been at work at the same time, making it difficult to parse out the effects of quantitative easing on the economy.

Nevertheless, our estimated term-structure model for Japan does suggest that yields in Japan were noticeably lower during the quantitative easing period than would have been predicted by the model, a bit of evidence for the effectiveness of this policy. A similar result emerges for the period of the Bank of Japan's zero-interest-rate policy, suggesting that the event study analysis may not have captured the full effect of the BOJ's policy commitments on longer-term yields.

Despite our relatively encouraging findings concerning the potential efficacy of non-standard policies at the zero bound, we remain cautious about making policy prescriptions. Although it appears that non-standard policy measures may affect asset yields and thus potentially the economy, considerable uncertainty remains about the size and reliability of these effects under the circumstances prevailing near the zero bound. Thus, we still believe the best policy approach is avoidance by maintaining a sufficient inflation buffer and easing preemptively as necessary to minimize the risk of hitting the ZLB. However, in the case of the unavoidable, we hope that our research will provide some guidance on the potential of nonstandard policies to lift the economy away from the zero bound.

Monetary Policy Options at the Zero Bound

It is not without some irony that the resurgence in work on the ZLB, which for more than a few generations of economists seemed to be a relic of the Depression era, traces to a remarkable achievement by central banks in the major industrial economies. Among those countries, consumer price inflation has fallen to around 2 percent, about one-third the pace of twenty years ago.[2] For instance, as shown in figure 1, the median

inflation rate among 27 countries labeled "advanced" in the International Monetary

Fund's *World Economic Outlook* database has moved down steadily since 1980.[3] This

disciplined pursuit of low inflation has no doubt generated macroeconomic benefits and

should be considered a singular accomplishment, but it also has been associated with

episodes of very low inflation and, sometimes, outright deflation.[4] The minimum

inflation rate observed among the 27 large economies in this sample has often been

negative—and consistently so over the past ten years. In the case of Japan, deflation over

the past five years implies that the current level of consumer prices is now the same as in

1995.

[FIGURE 1 ABOUT HERE]

With inflation low and likely to remain so, industrial countries are at risk of

encountering the zero bound on nominal interest rates periodically in the future. This

raises the stakes for answering the question: What options exist for monetary policy

when lowering the nominal short-term interest rate, the usual response to a weak

economy, is no longer available? Possible answers to this question have been discussed

in many previous essays, and we will not review this extensive literature in detail here.

Instead, as background for the empirical results to be presented later in the paper, we

provide an overview that focuses on some key debates about the effectiveness of

---

[2] October of this year marks an important turning point in those efforts: Twenty-five-years ago, Paul
Volcker and the other members of the Federal Open Market Committee fired the initial salvo in the battle
to conquer inflation.
[3] Data from Iceland and Israel, which both experienced bouts of very high inflation, are excluded from the
sample as they distort the maximums shown in the figure.
[4] Key references on the benefits, and possible costs, of low inflation include Friedman (1969), Feldstein
(1997), and Akerlof, Dickens, and Perry (1996).

**Figure 1. Consumer price inflation in advanced economies,
1980 to 2005**

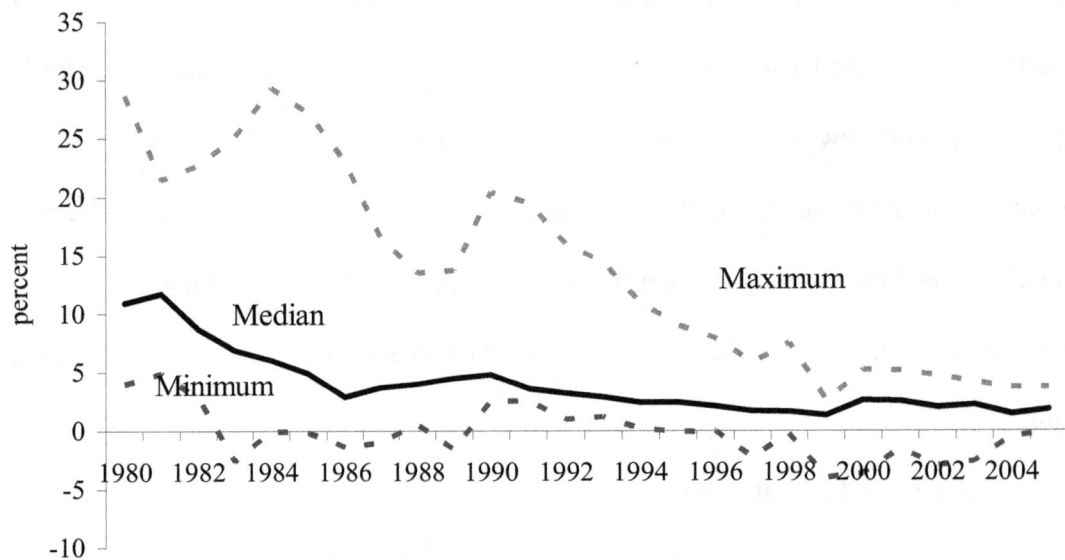

Source: International Monetary Fund, World Economic Outlook (April 2004); IMF definition of 28 advanced economies excluding Iceland and Israel.

alternative non-standard policies and describes existing empirical evidence bearing on these debates.

Bernanke and Reinhart (2004) discuss three alternative, though potentially complementary, strategies when monetary policymakers are confronted with a short-term nominal interest rate that is close to zero. As discussed in the introduction, these alternatives involve (1) shaping the expectations of the public about future settings of the policy rate, (2) increasing the size of the central bank's balance sheet beyond the level needed to set the short-term policy rate at zero ("quantitative easing"); and (3) shifting the composition of the central bank's balance sheet in order to affect the relative supplies of securities held by the public. We use this taxonomy here as well to organize our discussion of non-standard policy options at or near the zero bound.

Shaping policy expectations

Commentators often describe the stance of a central bank's policy in terms of the level of the short-term nominal interest rate. For example, the very low short-term rates seen in Japan in recent years have led many to refer to the Bank of Japan's monetary policy as "ultra-easy." However, associating the stance of policy entirely with the level of the short-term nominal interest rate can be seriously misleading. At a minimum, a distinction needs to be drawn between the nominal short-term rate and the real short-term rate; in a deflationary environment, a nominal interest rate near zero does not preclude the possibility that real interest rates are too high for the health of the economy.

A more subtle reason that the level of the policy rate does not fully describe the stance of monetary policy is that a given policy rate may coexist with widely varying configurations of asset prices and yields, and hence with varying degrees of policy stimulus broadly considered. In the United States, at least, the short-term policy rate has little direct effect on private-sector borrowing and investment decisions. Rather, those decisions respond most sensitively to longer-term yields (such as the yields on mortgages and corporate bonds) and to the prices of long-lived assets (such as equities). A given short-term rate may thus be associated with relatively restrictive financial conditions (for example, if the term structure were sharply upward sloping and equity prices depressed), or alternatively with relatively easy conditions (if the term structure were flat or downward sloping and equity prices high). Indeed, copious research by financial economists has demonstrated that two and possibly three factors (sometimes referred to as level, slope, and curvature) are needed to describe the term structure of interest rates, implying that the short-term policy rate alone can never be sufficient to describe fully the term structure, let alone the broad range of financial conditions.

Financial theory also tells us that the prices and yields of long-term assets, which play such an important role in the transmission of monetary policy, depend to a significant extent on financial market participants' expectations about the future path of short-term rates. In particular, with the relevant term, risk, and liquidity premiums held constant, expectations that short rates will be kept low will induce financial market participants to bid down long-term bond yields and (for given expectations about future corporate earnings) bid up the prices of equities. Because financial conditions depend on the expected future path of the policy rate as well as (or even more than) its current value, central bankers must be continuously aware of how their actions shape the public's policy expectations. The crucial role of expectations in the making of monetary policy, in normal times as well as when the policy rate is near the zero bound, has recently been stressed in important papers by Eggertsson and Woodford (2003a,b). Indeed, in the context of their theoretical model, Eggertsson and Woodford (henceforth EW) obtain the strong result that shaping the interest-rate expectations of the public is essentially the only tool that central bankers have—in normal conditions, as well as when the ZLB binds. We will have several occasions to refer to the EW result below and opportunities to suggest that the levers of policy are greater in number than they contend.

How then can a central bank influence private-sector expectations? EW, like most of the literature, emphasize the importance of the central bank's committing in advance to a policy rule. The focus is rightly on the problem of designing policy rules that perform reasonably well both close to and away from the zero bound. These authors are surely correct that predictable, "rule-like" behavior by central banks is an important means of shaping the public's policy expectations. Central banks have generally become more predictable in recent years, reflecting factors such as increased transparency and, in some cases, the adoption of explicit policy frameworks such as inflation targeting. However, there are limits in practice to the ability of central banks to commit "once and for all" to a fully specified policy rule, as envisioned by theoretical analyses of monetary policy "under commitment." While a theoretician might be able to specify the appropriate state-contingent policy plan for a given model, in practice, a central bank would likely find it particularly difficult to describe the details of its reactions to highly unusual circumstances, such as those associated with the policy rate being constrained by the zero bound.

Given that the ability to commit to precisely specified rules is limited, central bankers have found it useful in practice to supplement their actions with talk, communicating regularly with the public about the outlook for the economy and for policy. Even in normal times, such communication can be helpful in achieving a closer alignment between the policy expectations of the public and the plans of the central bank. If the central bank places a cost on being seen to renege on earlier statements, communication in advance may also enhance the central bank's ability to commit to certain policies or courses of action.

Although communication is always important, its importance may be elevated when the policy rate is constrained by the ZLB. In particular, even with the overnight rate at zero, the central bank may be able to impart additional stimulus to the economy by persuading the public that the policy rate will remain low for a longer period than was previously expected. One means of doing so would be to shade interest-rate expectations downward is by making a commitment to the public to follow a policy of extended monetary ease. This commitment, if credible and not previously expected, should lower longer-term rates, support other asset prices, and boost aggregate demand.

Bernanke and Reinhart (2004) note that, in principle, such commitments could be unconditional (that is, linked only to the calendar) or conditional (linked to developments in the economy). Unconditional commitments are rare. Perhaps the Federal Reserve's commitment to peg short-term and long-term rates during the decade after 1942, discussed below, might be considered an example of an unconditional commitment, in that the pegging operation was open-ended and did not specify an exit strategy. More usually, central bank commitments about future policies are explicitly conditional.

An important recent example of a conditional commitment is the zero-interest-rate-policy (ZIRP) of the Bank of Japan (BOJ). The BOJ's policy rate, the call rate, was reduced to a level "as low as possible"—to zero, for all practical purposes—in February 1999. In April 1999, describing the stance of monetary policy as "super super expansionary," then-Governor Hayami announced that the BOJ would keep the policy rate at zero "until deflationary concerns are dispelled," with the latter phrase clearly indicating that the policy commitment was conditional. However, in a case of what might be called commitment *interruptus*, the BOJ raised the call rate to 25 basis points in August 2000. Following a subsequent weakening in economic conditions, the rate increase was partly retracted in February 2001. The ZIRP was then effectively reinstated in March 2001 when the BOJ announced that it would henceforth target bank reserves at a level well above that needed to bring the call rate to zero (a policy of "quantitative easing"; see below). Since that time, the BOJ has attempted to assure the markets that the reconstituted ZIRP, together with its other extraordinary policy measures, will be maintained as long as deflation persists. Indeed, under Governor Fukui, the BOJ has become more explicit about the conditions required to move the call-money rate from its zero floor, asserting that ZIRP will not end until year-over-year core inflation has been positive for several months and, moreover, is expected to remain positive.

A relevant, though less explicit, example of policy commitment is also available for the United States. Federal Reserve officials expressed concerns about the "remote" possibility of deflation from the latter part of 2002 through much of 2003. Subsequently, in late 2003 and early 2004, though the deflation risk had receded, the slow pace of job creation exacerbated concerns about the recovery's sustainability. Although the Federal

Reserve's policy rate remained at least 100 basis points above zero throughout this period, policymakers became more specific in communicating their outlook for policy in the attempt to shape expectations. For example, the August 2003 statement of the Federal Open Market Committee (FOMC) that "policy accommodation can be maintained for a considerable period" may be interpreted as an example of conditional commitment.[5] The conditional nature of the commitment was made clear in the Committee's December 2003 policy statement, which explicitly linked continuing policy accommodation to the low level of inflation and slack in resource use. Likewise, the Committee's stated plan in 2004 to "remove policy accommodation at a pace that is likely to be measured" gave the market information about the likely direction of the policy rate but also emphasized that future actions would be linked explicitly to the condition that inflation remain under control.

Empirical evidence on the ability of central banks to influence policy expectations through statements, speeches, and other forms of "talk" is relatively limited. For the United States, Kohn and Sack (2003) present evidence that the issuance of FOMC statements increases the variability of market interest rates on the day of the statement, suggesting that these statements convey information to financial markets over and above the information in the policy action. However, they do not specifically address the ability of the FOMC to influence expectations of future policy in the desired direction or at longer horizons. In the next section, we extend the work of Kohn and Sack to provide additional evidence on the effects of FOMC statements on policy expectations and asset prices.

---

[5] The full text of the FOMC's statement can be found at www.federalreserve.gov/fomc

More work has been done on the effects of the BOJ's zero-interest-rate-policy, primarily by researchers at the Bank of Japan and affiliated research institutions. The majority of this research suggests that the ZIRP has been successful at affecting policy expectations and, thus, yields, though with the greatest impact at the short end of the maturity spectrum (Fujiki and Shiratsuka, 2002; Takeda and Yajima, 2002; Okina and Shiratsuka, 2003). Also, studies that include both the early ZIRP period, before August 2000, and the later application of the policy, which commenced in March 2001 with the introduction of the quantitative easing policy, tend to find modestly stronger effects in the latter period (Nagasayu, 2004). In an interesting paper, Marumo et al. (2003) use an estimated model of the Japanese term structure to back out the evolution of market participants' beliefs about how long the ZIRP would hold. They find that, over the period from February 1999 to August 2000, the mode of the probability distribution over the expected remaining time of the policy ranged from less than one year to about two years. For the second incarnation of the ZIRP, after March 2001, they find that modal expectations of the time to the end of the zero-interest-rate policy varied from approximately two to three years. Similar results were obtained by Okina and Shiratsuka (2004), who ultimately conclude that "[t]he policy duration effect was highly effective in stabilizing market expectations regarding the future path of short-term interest rates, thereby bringing longer-term interest rates down to flatten the yield curve."[6]

A shortcoming shared by most of the studies cited above, however, is the absence of an adequate benchmark for the term structure. That is, most existing studies do not

---

[6] However, Okina and Shiratsuka also argue that the ZIRP did not help the economy much, "since [the] transmission channel linking the financial and non-financial sectors has remained blocked."

14

effectively answer the question of what yields would have been in absence of the ZIRP. Hence, we really do not know (for example) whether the exceedingly low level of longer-term government bond yields in Japan during recent years primarily reflects expectations of low future policy rates or the belief that Japan faces a protracted period of deflation. In an interesting recent paper, Baba et al. (2004) address the benchmark issue by estimating a "macro-finance," no-arbitrage model of the term structure (as discussed in more detail in the next section). They use this model to estimate what yields in Japan would have been at each date, given the state of the economy and under the counterfactual assumption that no ZIRP was in place. A comparison of the actual term structure to the estimated benchmark permits inferences about the effects of the ZIRP. Notably, these authors find somewhat stronger net effects of the ZIRP on long-term yields than does much of the earlier work. We apply a similar strategy in our empirical analysis below.

Our discussion, like much of the literature, has focused on regimes in which the short-term nominal interest rate is the instrument of monetary policy. However, in principle, any nominal quantity could serve as a nominal anchor for the system and thus as a target or instrument for the central bank. Svensson (2001, 2003) has called attention to the nominal exchange rate as an alternative policy instrument when the ZLB binds, noting that monetary policies that can be defined in terms of current and future values of the short-term nominal interest rate can equally well be expressed in terms of paths for the nominal exchange rate. Switching the policy instrument from the short-term interest rate to the exchange rate does not eliminate the constraints imposed by the zero bound; some paths for the nominal exchange rate cannot be engineered by the central bank

15

because the values of the short-term nominal interest rate implied by interest-rate parity would violate the ZLB. Nevertheless, we agree with Svensson that commitments by the central bank to future policies may be more credible when expressed in terms of a planned path for the exchange rate rather than in terms of future values of the short-term nominal interest rate. One obvious benefit of expressing policy commitments in terms of the exchange rate is that it is verifiable, in that the central bank's announcement can be accompanied by an immediate and visible change in the exchange rate; whereas promises about future values of the short-term interest rate cannot be accompanied by immediate action, if the current policy rate is at the ZLB.

These considerations suggest that exchange-rate-based policies may be the best way for smaller open economies to break the hold of the ZLB. For example, the Swiss National Bank increased its use of the exchange rate as a policy indicator during its recent struggle with the ZLB. Whether exchange-rate-based policies can be used by large economies like the United States or Japan is more controversial. Opponents have argued that the strongest short-term effects of the exchange-rate devaluation suggested by Svensson would be felt on the patterns of trade, raising the possibility that the large country's trading partners would accuse it of following a "beggar-thy-neighbor" policy. Svensson has replied that growth in domestic demand would ultimately raise imports, offsetting the terms-of-trade effects created by the devaluation. Whether these second-round effects would develop quickly enough to help defuse the political problem, however, is difficult to judge, and we have nothing to add to this controversy. Because large industrial countries have traditionally emphasized interest rates and money growth as policy instruments, we focus on these variables in the remainder of the paper. That said, we believe that empirical study of the use of the exchange rate as a policy indicator when the ZLB is binding would be highly worthwhile.

Increasing the size of the central bank's balance sheet (quantitative easing)

Central banks normally lower their policy rate through open-market purchases of bonds or other securities, which have the effect of increasing the supply of bank reserves and putting downward pressure on the rate that clears the reserves market. A sufficient injection of reserves will bring the policy rate arbitrarily close to zero, so that the ZLB rules out further interest rate reduction. However, nothing prevents the central bank from adding liquidity to the system beyond what is needed to achieve a policy rate of zero, a policy that is know as quantitative easing. As already noted, Japan has actively pursued this policy approach in recent years. Announced in March 2001, the BOJ's quantitative easing policy (QEP) might have initially been interpreted as a re-commitment to the policy of keeping the short rate at zero, the ZIRP. However, the BOJ raised its target for current account balances at commercial banks (essentially, bank reserves) a number of times to the point that reserves substantially exceeded the level needed to pin the call rate at zero. (The BOJ's target for current account balances reached 30-35 trillion yen in January 2004, compared to required reserves of approximately 6 trillion yen, and the monetary base grew by two-thirds in the three years following the initiation of QEP (as reported in Baba et al, 2004)). However, as has been frequently noted, growth in bank reserves and base money in Japan have not resulted in comparable growth in broader monetary aggregates. In large part, this limited effect has been the result of the poor condition of banks' and borrowers' balance sheets, which makes profitable lending difficult and induces banks to hold large quantities of idle balances.

Whether quantitative easing can be effective in relieving deflationary pressures, and if so, by what mechanism, remains controversial. As already noted, EW have provided theoretical reasons to doubt the efficacy of quantitative easing as an independent tool of policy. Specifically, they show that, in a world in which financial frictions are limited and in which a clear dichotomy is maintained between monetary and fiscal policies, quantitative easing will have *no* effect, except perhaps to the extent that the extra money creation can be used to signal the central bank's intentions regarding future values of the short-term interest rate. The assumptions of frictionless financial markets and complete separation of monetary and fiscal policies, to be sure, are rather strong. If these assumptions do not hold, we may have some basis for believing that quantitative easing will be effective.

Why might injections of liquidity help the economy, even beyond the point necessary to drive the short-term policy rate to zero? One argument for quantitative easing that has been adopted by some proponents is what might be called the *reduced-form argument*. Broadly, those making this argument are agnostic about the precise mechanisms by which quantitative easing may have its effects. Instead, in support of quantitative easing as an anti-deflationary tool, they point to the undeniable fact that, historically, money growth and inflation have tended to be strongly associated. It follows, according to this argument, that money creation will raise prices independent of its effects on the term structure.

Basing policy recommendations on reduced-form evidence of this sort is problematic, however. As the Lucas critique warns us, historical relationships are prone to break down in novel circumstances. In particular, there is no reason to expect the velocity of money to be stable or predictable when the short-term interest rate (the opportunity cost of holding money) is close to zero, and thus no reason to expect a stable relationship between money growth and nominal income under those conditions. To make the case for quantitative easing, we need more explicit descriptions of how additional money growth might stimulate the economy even when the short-term interest rate has reached zero.

At least three channels through which quantitative easing may be effective have been advanced. First, a view associated both with monetarist expositions, such as Meltzer (2001), and Keynesian classics such as Brainard and Tobin (1968) and Tobin (1969), builds from the premise that money and other financial assets are imperfect substitutes. According to the imperfect substitutes view, increases in the money supply induce households and firms to try to rebalance their portfolios by trading money for non-money assets. Because the private sector collectively cannot change its asset holdings, attempts to rebalance portfolios will tend to raise the prices and lower the yields of non-money assets if money and non-money assets are imperfect substitutes. Higher asset values and lower yields in turn stimulate the economy, according to this view. Recently, Andres, Lopez-Salido, and Nelson (2003) have shown how these effects might work in a general equilibrium model that includes financial-market frictions.

So long as technology has not made it possible to pay a grocery bill with a stock certificate or the deed to a home, it is difficult to dispute the premise that, as a general matter, money and non-money assets are imperfect substitutes. However, in the special situation of a binding ZLB, large additional injections of liquidity may satiate the public's demand for money, implying that, on the margin, extra cash provides no transactions services to households or firms. If money demand is satiated, money becomes (on the margin) just another financial asset, one that happens to pay a zero nominal rate, to be riskless in nominal terms, and to have an indefinite maturity. In this situation, it is no longer obvious that money is a particularly bad substitute for non-monetary assets. For example, with the important exception of its maturity, money's characteristics are very close to those of short-term Treasury bills paying close to zero interest. Of course, even in this situation there will be assets—real estate for example—that are not very substitutable with money, implying that the central bank's choice of assets to buy may matter a great deal.

A second possible channel for quantitative easing to influence the economy is the fiscal channel. This channel relies on the observation that sufficiently large monetary injections will materially relieve the government's budget constraint, permitting tax reductions or increases in government spending without increasing public holdings of government debt (Bernanke, 2003; Auerbach and Obstfeld, 2004). Effectively, the fiscal channel is based on the government's substitution of the inflation tax (a tax with little or no deadweight loss in a deflationary environment) for direct taxes such as income taxes. Auerbach and Obstfeld (2004) provide a detailed analysis of both the macroeconomic and welfare effects of the fiscal channel and find that these effects are potentially quite substantial. These authors also note, however, that the fiscal effect of quantitative easing will be attenuated or absent if the public expects today's monetary injections to be withdrawn in the future.[7] Broadly, if the public expects quantitative easing to be reversed at the first sign that deflation has ended, they will likewise expect that their money-financed tax cuts will be replaced by future tax increases as money is withdrawn, an expectation that will blunt the initial impact of the policy. Thus, it is crucial that the central bank's promises to maintain some part of its quantitative easing as the economy recovers be perceived as credible by the public. Auerbach and Obstfeld show that, if the central bank is known to be willing to tolerate even a very small amount of inflation, the promise to maintain quantitative easing will be credible. A similar result would likely obtain if the central bank associates even a relatively small cost with publicly reneging on its promises. Thus, it seems reasonable to expect that the fiscal channel of quantitative easing would work if pursued sufficiently aggressively.

A third potential channel of quantitative easing, admittedly harder to pin down than others, might be called the signalling channel. Simply put, quantitative easing may complement the expectations management approach by providing a visible signal to the public about the central bank's intended future policies. For example, if the public believes that the central bank will be hesitant to reverse large amounts of quantitative easing very quickly, perhaps because of the possible shock to money markets, this policy provides a way of underscoring the central bank's commitment to keeping the policy rate at zero for an extended period.

More speculatively, quantitative easing may work through a signalling channel if its implementation marks a general willingness of the central bank to break from the cautious and conventional policies of the past. An historical episode that may illustrate

---

[7] Their point is closely related to Krugman's (1998) important analysis, which emphasized the crucial role of central bank credibility in most non-conventional monetary policies.

this channel at work (although the policymaker in question was the executive rather than the central bank) was the period following Franklin Roosevelt's inauguration as U.S. president in 1933. During 1933 and 1934, the extreme deflation seen earlier in the decade suddenly reversed, stock prices jumped, and the economy grew rapidly. Romer (1992) has argued persuasively that this surprisingly sharp recovery was closely associated with rapid growth in the money supply that arose from Roosevelt's devaluation of the dollar, capital inflows from an increasingly unstable Europe, and other factors. As short-term interest rates remained near zero throughout the period, the episode is reasonably characterized as a successful application of quantitative easing. Romer (1992) does not explain the mechanism by which quantitative easing worked in this episode, other than to observe that real interest rates declined as deflation changed to inflation.[8] Temin and Wigmore (1990) addressed that question, arguing that the key to the sudden reversal was the public's acceptance of the idea that Roosevelt's policies constituted a "regime change." Unlike the policymakers who preceded him showing little inclination to resist deflation and, indeed, seeming to prefer deflation to even a small probability of future inflation, Roosevelt demonstrated clearly through his actions that he was committed to ending deflation and "reflating" the economy. Although the president could have simply announced his desire to raise prices, his adoption of policies that his predecessors would have considered reckless provided a powerful signal to the public that the economic situation had fundamentally changed. If one accepts the Temin-

---

[8] Dollar devaluation of course improved the competitiveness of U.S. exports and raised the prices of imports. But, in an economy that was by this time largely closed, the direct effects of devaluation seem unlikely to have been large enough to account for the sharp turnaround.

Wigmore hypothesis, then it appears that the signal afforded by Roosevelt's exchange-rate and monetary policies were central to the conquest of deflation in 1933-34.[9]

Outside of the suggestive evidence from the interwar period just discussed, there has been little empirical analysis of the quantitative easing channel. The only recent experience to draw upon, of course, is that of Japan since March 2001. Shirakawa (2002) reviewed the quantitative easing policy after one year and argued that, although the QEP may be credited with reducing liquidity premiums in some markets, it did not have discernible effects on the prices of most assets, including government bonds, the stock market, or the exchange rate, nor did it increase bank lending. Kimura et al. (2002) study the effects of quantitative easing by vector autoregression methods and by estimating a money demand equation. They conclude that any effects of quantitative easing have been very small and highly uncertain.

The facts that, recently, deflation has moderated in Japan and signs of recovery have appeared are of course a bit of evidence in favor of the effectiveness of BOJ's quantitative easing policy. Unfortunately, they are far from decisive. Other factors have certainly played a role in the recent improvement in the Japanese economy, including structural and banking reforms, a strengthening world economy, and the zero-interest-rate policy. The quantitative easing policy, although an important departure from the standard policy framework, has in fact been somewhat conservative in its execution. Despite some interesting initiatives intended to promote the development of various financial markets, the BOJ has largely restricted its open-market purchases to the usual suspects—government securities—thereby inhibiting any effect that might work through imperfect

[9] Meltzer (1999) has also drawn on the experience of the first half of the twentieth century, including episodes in 1920-21, 1937-38, and 1947-48, to argue for the potential benefits of quantitative easing.

substitutability. Even more important, there has been a notable absence of cooperation between the monetary and fiscal authorities (indeed, the BOJ has expressed repeated concerns that monetary ease might facilitate fiscal indiscipline), and the communication and signaling aspects of policy have been subdued. We present some evidence below that is consistent with quantitative easing having been effective in Japan, but it does not clearly isolate the effects of quantitative easing from other influences. The reality may well be that the Japanese experience does not provide strong conclusions about the potential efficacy of this particular non-standard policy.

Altering the composition of the central bank's balance sheet

The composition of the assets on the central bank's balance sheet offers another potential lever for monetary policy. For example, the Federal Reserve participates in all segments of the Treasury market, including inflation-indexed Treasury debt, with its asset holdings of about $695 billion distributed among Treasury securities with original maturities ranging from four weeks to thirty years. Over the past fifty years, the average maturity of the System's holdings of Treasury debt has varied considerably within a range from one to four years. By buying and selling securities of various maturities or other characteristics in the open market, the Fed could materially influence the relative supplies of these securities. In a frictionless financial market, as pointed out by EW, these changes in supply would have essentially no effect, as the pricing of any financial asset would depend exclusively on its state- and date-contingent payoffs. However, in a world with transactions costs and in which financial markets are incomplete in important ways, the Fed's action might be able to influence term, risk, and liquidity premiums—and thus overall yields.[10] The feasibility of this approach is, of course, closely related to the issue

 of whether types of assets are imperfect substitutes, as discussed earlier.

The same logic would apply, of course, to other financial and real assets that might be bought and sold by the central bank. Unless it were to invoke some emergency provisions dormant since the 1930s, however, the Federal Reserve is restricted to purchasing a limited range of assets outside of Treasury securities, including some foreign government bonds, the debt of government-sponsored enterprises, and some municipal securities. These restrictions might effectively be made less binding by various methods. For example, the Fed has the authority to accept a wide range of assets for collateral for discount-window loans. Some other central banks face fewer restrictions on the assets they can hold; for example, the Bank of Japan's expansionary efforts have involved purchases not only treasury bills and Japanese government bonds (JGBs), but also commercial paper, various asset-backed securities, and equities (from commercial banks).

Perhaps the most extreme example of a policy keyed to the composition of the central bank's balance sheet is the announcement of a ceiling on some longer-term yield, below the rate initially prevailing in the market. Such a policy would entail an essentially unlimited commitment to purchase the targeted security at the announced price. (If these purchases are allowed to affect the size of the central bank's balance sheet as well as its composition, ultimately the policy might also involve quantitative easing. A "pure"

---

[10] In carrying out such a policy, the Fed would need to coordinate with the Treasury, to ensure that Treasury debt issuance policies did not offset the Fed's actions.

pegging policy would require the central bank to sell other securities equal in amount to its purchases of the targeted security.)

As with quantitative easing, whether policies based on manipulating the composition of the central bank's balance sheet can have significant effects is contentious. Again, the benchmark "frictionless" market of financial markets predicts no effect. A fair characterization of the prevailing view among financial economists is that changes in the relative supplies of assets within the range of U.S. experience are unlikely to have a major impact on these premiums and thus on overall yields.[11] We will present new evidence on this issue later in the paper. If the view that financial pricing approximates the frictionless ideal is correct, then attempts to enforce a ceiling on the yields of long-term Treasury securities would be successful only if the targeted yields were broadly consistent with investor expectations about future values of the policy rate. If investors doubted that rates would be kept low, this view would predict that the central bank would end up owning all or most of the targeted security. Moreover, even if large purchases of, say, a long-dated Treasury security were able to affect the yield on that security, the possibility exists that the yield on that security might become "disconnected" from the rest of the term structure and from private rates, thus reducing the economic impact of the policy.

Theoretical objections notwithstanding, there are a number of historical examples of rate pegs by central banks. During the twentieth century, central banks in a number of countries successfully pegged (or imposed a ceiling on) long-term government bond rates

---

[11] Reinhart and Sack (2000) show that a simple mean-variance model of portfolio choice predicts that even sizable changes in the composition of the public's asset holding would have only small effects on yields. However, we should note that evidence of imperfect substitution among broad asset classes has been provided in a number of studies, including Roley (1987) and Friedman and Kuttner (1998).

in order to facilitate the financing of war or postwar reconstruction. In the United States, the Federal Reserve maintained ceilings on Treasury yields at seven maturities between 1942 and the 1951 Accord, among them caps of 3/8 percent on ninety-day Treasury bill rates (raised to ¾ percent in July 1947) and of 2-1/2 percent on very long-term bonds. The peg on bills appeared to be binding, in that for most of the period the rate on bills remained precisely at the announced level, while Fed holdings of bills grew steadily, exceeding 90 percent of the outstanding stock by 1947 (Toma, 1992). In contrast, the 2-1/2 percent cap on long-term bond yields was maintained without active intervention throughout much of the period, suggesting that the cap was not a binding constraint. There were exceptions to this generalization, however: Notably, from the beginning of the regime in April 1942 through December 1944, long-term bond yields fluctuated in a narrow range between 2.43 percent and 2.50 percent, suggesting some influence of the cap (Hutchinson and Toma, 1991). Also, between October 1947 and December 1948, the Fed appears to have intervened actively to keep bond yields just below the peg, in the process raising the central bank's holdings of bonds from near zero to about 13 percent of the outstanding stock (Toma, 1992).

The relative ease with which the Fed maintained the ceiling on long-term government bond yields for an entire decade raises intriguing questions. During the early part of the pegging period, memories of the low interest rates of the 1930s and ongoing low inflation (enforced in part by wartime price controls) plausibly implied equilibrium long-term yields either below or not far above the Fed's ceiling. After the war and the elimination of wartime controls, however, inflation rose quite sharply. Yet the long-term peg remained intact. Eichengreen and Garber (1991) argue that the public was confident that the Fed would reverse the postwar inflation and hence remained content to hold low-yielding bonds. Likewise, Toma (1992) notes that there is no logical inconsistency in promising a monetary policy that is easy in the short run but anti-inflationary in the long run, as the Fed's pegging policy seemed to do. In the present paper we focus our empirical analysis on more recent episodes, and so we confine ourselves here to raising a few questions about the pre-Accord period that we believe merit further analysis. First, if we accept the Eichengreen-Garber argument that long-term inflation expectations were well-behaved during this period, we might still ask how if at all the Fed's pegging policy influenced those expectations. For example, did the pegging policy communicate a commitment to low inflation, perhaps because the public understood that the Fed would do all it could to avert the capital losses to banks and on its own account that would be suffered if inflation and long-term rates rose sharply? Second, did the pegging policy affect term premiums, for example, by reducing the perceived risk in holding long-term bonds? Finally, did the Fed in fact succeed in pegging long-term yields below their equilibrium levels in 1942-44 and 1947-48, and if so, what were the consequences?

A second well-known historical episode involving the attempted manipulation of the term structure was the so-called Operation Twist. Launched in early 1961 by the incoming Kennedy administration, Operation Twist was intended to raise short-term rates (thereby promoting capital inflows and supporting the dollar) while lowering, or at least not raising, long-term rates (Modigliani and Sutch, 1966). The two main actions underlying Operation Twist were the use of Federal Reserve open-market operations and Treasury debt management operations to shorten the average maturity of government debt held by the public; and some easing of the rate restrictions on deposits imposed by

Regulation Q. Operation Twist is widely viewed today as having been a failure, largely due to the classic work by Modigliani and Sutch (1966, 1967).[12] Empirical estimates of the "habitat model" of interest-rate determination by these authors led them to conclude that Operation Twist narrowed the long-short spread by amounts that "are most unlikely to exceed some ten to twenty base points—a reduction that can be considered moderate at best (1966, p. 196)." However, Modigliani and Sutch also noted that Operation Twist was a relatively small operation, and, indeed, that over a slightly longer period the maturity of outstanding government debt rose significantly, rather than falling (supporting Tobin's gloomy assessment noted in the footnote). Thus, Operation Twist does not seem to provide strong evidence in either direction as to the possible effects of changes in the composition of the central bank's balance sheet. In the next section, we will consider the effects of more significant changes in relative supplies of government bonds of different maturities than were observed during Operation Twist.

The Potential Effectiveness of Non-Standard Policies: Evidence from the United States

Although the federal funds rate declined to 1 percent in 2003, short-term nominal interest rates in the United States have not been effectively constrained by the zero lower bound since the 1930s. Nevertheless, the recent experience of the United States provides some opportunities to test the potential effectiveness of non-standard monetary policies in a modern, financially sophisticated economy.

---

[12] The Modigliani-Sutch conclusion was not uncontroversial; see for example Holland (1969). Indeed, Tobin asserts that Treasury debt management undercut any effects that might have followed from the relatively small change in the composition of the Federal Reserve's balance sheet (Tobin, 1974, pp. 32-33).

The previous section classified non-standard monetary policies under three headings: (1) using communications to shape policy expectations, (2) increasing the size of the central bank's balance sheet beyond what is needed to bring short-term rates to zero (quantitative easing); and (3) changing the composition of the central bank's in order to affect the relative supplies, and thus possibly the relative prices, of targeted securities. As far as we can see, the recent experience of the United States does not contain any episodes useful for studying the potential of quantitative easing, the second type of nonstandard policy. However, as we discuss in this section, recent U.S. experience does provide valuable evidence, both direct and indirect, on the effectiveness of the first and third classes of non-standard monetary policies.

We first address the question of whether the recent communication policies of the Federal Open Market Committee (FOMC), the committee responsible for monetary policy in the United States, have influenced market expectations of future short-term interest rates, as would be required to affect longer-term rates by shaping market expectations (the first class of non-standard policies). Our principal methodology is event-study analysis; that is, we draw inferences about the impact of FOMC statements from the behavior of market-based indicators of policy expectations in a short window surrounding FOMC announcements. We also use the event-study approach to determine whether FOMC statements affect the responsiveness of policy expectations to other types of news, such as employment reports. The event-study analysis shows that FOMC policy statements do in fact have a substantial impact on the markets' expectations of future policy, both directly and indirectly, suggesting that the Committee does have some scope to use communications policies to influence yields and prices of longer-term assets. To assess further the magnitude of these effects, we next estimate a "macro-finance" model of the term structure of Treasury yields, which links the term structure to macroeconomic conditions and to indicators of monetary policy. Comparison of this benchmark model of the term structure to the actual evolution of yields provides additional information on the magnitude and duration of the effects of FOMC "talk" on the term structure.

In the second part of this section, we present evidence that bears on the possibility that changes in the composition of the Fed's balance sheet might influence asset prices (the third class of non-standard policy). The key issue here is whether changes in the relative supplies of assets, such as government bonds of different maturities, have significant effects on prices and yields, holding constant macroeconomic conditions and policy interest rates. We address this issue indirectly by considering the market effects of three recent episodes: (1) the period of Treasury "buybacks", during which the Treasury announced its attentions to shorten significantly the maturity structure of U.S. debt; (2) the large purchases of U.S. Treasuries by Japan's Ministry of Finance during the period of Japan's exchange-rate interventions; and (3) the "deflation scare" episode of 2003, during which bond-market participants purportedly placed significant probability that the Fed might use bond purchases to try to affect longer-term yields. Using the same two methodologies as applied in the study of FOMC statements—that is, an event-study approach and the use of an estimated model of the term structure as a benchmark for comparison—we find evidence that "supply effects" have, at times, significantly influenced bond yields, suggesting that targeted purchases of bonds at the zero bound could be effective at lowering the yields on longer-dated securities. However, the duration and magnitude of these effects remains somewhat unclear from our analysis.

Do FOMC statements influence policy expectations?

Has the Federal Reserve's policymaking body, the Federal Open Market Committee, historically exerted any influence on investors' expectations about the future course of policy? Although members of the FOMC communicate to the public through a variety of channels, including speeches and Congressional testimonies, official communications from the Committee as an official body (*ex cathedra*, one might say) are confined principally to the statements that the FOMC releases with its policy decisions.[13],[14] In this section we investigate whether FOMC statements have observable effects on financial markets, over and above the effects of policy changes themselves. Later in the paper we undertake a similar exercise for the Bank of Japan.

The FOMC has moved significantly in the direction of greater transparency over the past decade. Before 1994, no policy statements or description of the target for the federal funds rate were released after FOMC meetings. Instead, except when changes in the federal funds rate coincided with changes in the discount rate (which were announced by a press release of the Federal Reserve Board), the Committee only signaled its policy decisions to the financial markets indirectly through the Desk's open market operations, typically on the day following the policy decision. In February 1994, the FOMC began to release statements to note changes in its target for the federal funds rate but continued to remain silent following meetings with no policy changes. Since May 1999, however, the Committee has released a statement after every policy meeting.

---

[13] Speeches and testimony by members of the Board of Governors, as well as FOMC statements, minutes, and transcripts, are available on the Federal Reserve's public website, www.federalreserve.gov.

[14] Some testimony, notably the Chairman's semi-annual report to Congress, might also be interpreted as reflecting the collective views of the Committee. Speeches by the Chairman are not technically official communications but, because of the Chairman's influence on policy decisions, are watched carefully by market participants.

The FOMC statements have evolved considerably. In their most recent form, they provide a brief description of the current state of the economy and, in some cases, some hints about the near-term outlook for policy. They also contain a formulaic description of the so-called "balance of risks" with respect to the outlook for output growth and inflation. A consecutive reading of the statements reveals continual tinkering by the Committee to improve its communications. For example, the balance-of-risks portion of the statement replaced an earlier formulation, the so-called "policy tilt", which characterized the likely future direction of the federal funds rate. Much like the "tilt" statement, the balance of risks statement hints about the likely evolution of policy, but it does so more indirectly by focusing on the Committee's assessment of the potential risks to its dual objectives rather than on the policy rate. The relative weights of "forward-looking" and "backward-looking" characterizations of the data and of policy have also changed over time, with the Committee taking a relatively more forward-looking stance in 2003 and 2004.

Of course, investors read the statements carefully to try to divine the Committee's views on the economy and its policy inclinations.[15] Investors' careful attention to the statements is *prima facie* evidence that what the Committee says, as well as what it does, matters for asset pricing. Here, we support this observation with more formal evidence and try to judge the magnitude of the effect.

To measure the extent of the influence of these FOMC announcements, we first take an event-study approach. We look at the movements in three market-based indicators of the private sector's monetary policy expectations during the periods

---

[15] It has been said that a mark of great literature is that readers can find meanings in the text that the author did not consciously intend. On this criterion, FOMC statements certainly qualify as great literature.

surrounding FOMC decisions—including both decisions taken at scheduled FOMC meetings and decisions taken between regular meetings—since July 1991.[16] The first of the three indicators is a now-standard measure of the surprise component of current policy decisions. This measure, derived from the current-month federal funds futures contract in the manner described by Kuttner (2001), provides a market-based estimate of the difference between the federal funds target set by the Committee and the value of the funds rate target that was expected by market participants just before the Committee's announcement. The second indicator is the rate on the Eurodollar futures contract expiring about a year ahead. Roughly speaking, the change in this rate during the period that spans the announcement of the FOMC's decision is a measure of the change in year-ahead policy expectations (and movements in the risk premium associated with those changes) induced by the Committee's decisions. Finally, we also consider changes in the yield on Treasury securities of five years' maturity, which provide an indication of changes in market expectations of policy (as well as associated changes in risk premiums) at a five-year horizon.[17] To isolate the effects of policy events on these indicators as cleanly as possible, we focus on movements in the three market-based indicators over the one-hour window (from fifteen minutes before to forty-five minutes after) surrounding the policy announcements

We would like to test whether the private-sector's policy expectations over the hour surrounding an FOMC announcement are affected solely by the unexpected component of the policy action itself, or whether there is room for additional influences

---

[16] Determining precisely when each decision was conveyed or signaled to the markets is a tedious process. See the text and especially the appendix of Gürkaynak, Sack, and Swanson (2004) for a discussion and a detailed listing of the timing of decisions.

[17] We measure the five-year yield as a zero-coupon yield, which in turn is derived from a smoothed yield-curve series maintained at the Federal Reserve Board.

on expectations arising from the Committee's statement. The prior literature has mostly considered the effects on asset prices and yields of the current policy surprise only (Kuttner, 2001; Bernanke and Kuttner, forthcoming). If the "one-factor" view of the effects of FOMC decisions implicit in these studies is correct, then there can be no independent effect of the Committee's statements on policy expectations or asset prices. To investigate this issue, we follow an approach similar to that of Gürkaynak, Sack, and Swanson (2004) to determine whether significant factors independent of the current policy surprise are needed to account for the response of policy expectations at the one-year and five-year horizons.[18] Specifically, we construct a candidate set of factors through a Cholesky decomposition of our three indicators of changes in policy expectations. We assume the first factor equals the current policy surprise, as inferred from the federal funds futures market, which also affects the year-ahead future rate and the five-year yield. The second candidate factor equals the portion of the change in year-ahead policy expectations (as measured by the change in Eurodollar futures) not explained by (that is, orthogonal to) the first factor, which is also allowed to influence the five-year yield. As a residual, the third candidate factor is the change in the five-year Treasury yield not explained by (orthogonal to) the first two factors. If the "one-factor" view of the effects of policy decisions is correct, then the second and third candidate factors should account for only a small portion of the changes in longer-horizon interest

---

[18] Our analysis extends the work of Gurkaynak, Sack, and Swanson (2004) in two ways. First, we analyze the relationship of the policy factors to FOMC statements in greater detail. Second, as discussed later in the paper, we will extend the analysis to the case of Japan. Methodologically, our approach also differs some from theirs in some respects. In particular, GSS use four futures contracts covering policy expectations out to a year; we use only one contract to measure year-ahead expectations but use a longer-term yield as well. In addition, we use different methods than GSS to identify the underlying factors.

rates in the period surrounding FOMC decisions, and they should be unrelated to aspects of the FOMC decision (such as the statement) other than the change in the policy rate.

The loadings of the three market indicators of policy expectations on the three factors, as determined by the Cholesky decomposition, are shown in table 1a. By construction the diagonal elements of the table equal unity. As already noted, the first factor has been set equal to the surprise component in the current policy decision, as measured by the method of Kuttner (2001). Note that the second and third elements of the first column show the effect of a one-unit increase in the current policy surprise on policy expectations one year and five years ahead, respectively. As found by Kuttner (2001), the effects of a current policy surprise on yields diminish as the horizon lengthens. The second factor has (by design) a unitary effect on year-ahead policy expectations and diminishing effect on the five-year yield, while the third factor (by design) affects only the five-year yield.

[Table 1 about here]

An important finding is that the second factor (defined as the part of the change in the year-ahead rate that is orthogonal to the surprise in the funds rate) plays a substantial role in determining policy expectations. This point can be seen in table 1b, which reports the standard deviation of the effect of each factor on the three market indicators of expectations in the period since 1998.[19] The standard deviation of the component of the year-ahead futures rate accounted for by the second factor (10.1) is twice that of the component accounted for by the first factor (5.1). Putting the results in terms of variances, we can infer from table 1b that only about one-fifth of the variance in the year-

---

[19] The post-April 1998 subsample in Table 1b is chosen for comparability to the results presented below for the Bank of Japan. The results reported in the table are similar if the full sample is used.

Table 1. United States: Decomposition of policy indicators into factors

a. Loadings of market-based policy indicators on candidate factors

Effect of factor on:	*First factor*	*Second factor*	*Third factor*
Current policy setting	1.00	0.00	0.00
Year-ahead futures rate	0.51	1.00	0.00
Five-year yield	0.27	0.64	1.00

b. Contributions of factors to the standard deviations of policy indicators

Standard deviation of the effect of factor on:	*First factor*	*Second factor*	*Third factor*
Current policy setting	10.0	0	0
Year-ahead futures rate	5.1	10.1	0
Five-year yield	2.7	6.5	3.5

Note: Standard deviations are measured in basis points. The sample period for Table 1b is April 1998 through the present, for comparability with results presented later on for Japan.

ahead futures rate in the hour around policy decisions is explained by current policy surprises (the first factor), with the other four-fifths of the variance being captured by the second factor. This result confirms a primary conclusion of Gürkaynak, Sack, and Swanson (2004), who argue that two factors are needed to explain the influence of FOMC announcements on monetary policy expectations out to a horizon of a year.

Also significant is the finding that the second factor makes the largest contribution to the variability in the five-year Treasury yield during the hour around FOMC decisions. In terms of standard deviations, the contribution of the second factor to the variation in the five-year yield is about twice that of either the first or third factors. In terms of variances, the second factor accounts for 68 percent of the variability of the five-year yield during the event window, while the first factor explains 12 percent and the third factor explains 20 percent of the variance of the five-year yield.

Having determined that policy expectations are determined to an important degree by a second factor that represents influences on market expectations of policy not captured in the policy decision itself, we next ask whether the second factor is related to the FOMC's communications.[20] Informal inspection of the historical realizations of the various factors reveals that the second factor has become increasingly important in the latter part of the sample—the period when policy statements came into regular use. Even during the years from 1994 to 1999, when policy statements were used more sporadically, many of the large realizations of the second factor coincided with policy statements. In contrast, larger realizations of the first and third factors do not seem to line up with dates of policy statements.

---

[20] Gurkaynak, Sack, and Swanson (2004) also address this issue and conclude that the second factor is indeed related to FOMC statements.

To investigate more formally the link between FOMC statements and the three factors, we follow an approach similar to that employed by Kohn and Sack (2003). As described in the previous section, Kohn and Sack showed that, for given values of the policy surprise, the issuance of statements by the FOMC increases the variability of market interest rates, suggesting that statements contain information relevant to financial markets. Here we extend their approach in several ways, in part by examining the effects on expectations of different types of statements (including "anticipated" and "unanticipated" statements), by linking statements to policy expectations at differing horizons (as summarized by the three factors), and by checking whether the "directional" effects of policy statements on policy expectations seem reasonable.[21]

As a first step, in analogy to Kohn and Sack (2003), we regress the squared values of each of the factors on several dummy variable related to policy statements. The idea is to determine whether statements "matter" for policy expectations at different horizons, as summarized by the three factors, without having to quantify the statements. We define the first dummy (STATEMENT) to be one on any date on which the FOMC released a policy statement, zero otherwise. A positive estimated coefficient on STATEMENT implies that this particular factor tends to be larger in magnitude on dates on which a statement is released. Of the 116 policy decisions in our sample, 56 were accompanied by statements.

Of course, a statement that was fully anticipated by market participants would not be expected to generate a market reaction. With this in mind, we define a second dummy variable (STATEMENT SURPRISE) that equals one on dates on which the issued

---

[21] Also, unlike Kohn and Sack (2003), who use daily data, we continue to use intraday data.

statement included important information about the state of the economy or the path of monetary policy that was not expected by a substantial portion of market participants.

Obviously, assigning values to STATEMENT SURPRISE involves some subjectivity, as investors' expectations of statements cannot be quantified as easily as their expectations for settings of the policy rate. To construct this dummy variable, we read a set of commentaries written before and after each statement was released to determine whether the statement was substantially as expected by market participants or instead surprised the markets. "After-the-fact" commentaries that we examined included internal staff analyses from both the Federal Reserve Bank of New York and the Board of Governors of market reactions to the policy decision and the statement, as well as next-day articles about the FOMC's decision from the *Wall Street Journal*. A drawback of relying on after-the-fact analyses to determine which statements were "surprises," of course, is that the authors' interpretations may have been influenced, consciously or unconsciously, by the observed market responses.[22] To guard against this source of bias, we also used several "before-the-fact" sources, including (1) a pre-FOMC-meeting survey about expectations for the balance-of-risks (or policy bias) part of the statement conducted by Money Market Services and its successor Action Economics; (2) commentaries put out just before each meeting by a leading financial firm that specializes in monitoring FOMC action; and (3) the results of a survey conducted by the Federal Reserve Bank of New York that asks primary dealers about their expectations for the

---

[22] Although written after the fact, the Federal Reserve staff analyses not infrequently reported that the market's reaction was different from their *ex ante* assessment of the likely response, suggesting that the "retrospective bias" may not have been severe.

statement.[23] We took all occasions when the policy bias or the balance of risks differed from the median survey response as surprises. Using these materials, we identified 31 of the 56 statements in our sample period as involving some non-negligible surprise. The breakdown of statements into surprises and non-surprises together with brief commentary is provided in an appendix that will be provided on request.

The regression results are presented in table 2 (for now, focus on columns 1, 3, and 5). Column 1 shows the results from regressing the square of the first factor (the current policy surprise) against a constant term and the two dummies. We observe that the dummy that indicates the presence of any statement (STATEMENT) appears with a positive and significant coefficient. The most likely explanation for this result is that, for much of the sample, statements were released only on days on which the federal funds rate was changed; not surprisingly, policy rate surprises tend to be larger in magnitude on days on which the federal funds rate target was changed, relative to days on which no change in the target was made. The coefficient on the dummy variable STATEMENT SURPRISE is negative and significant, which suggests that the FOMC views surprises in the policy rate and in the statement as substitutes, or possibly that the FOMC was simply reluctant to issue surprising statements at the same time that it was also surprising the markets with its policy action.

[Table 2 about here]

The regression reported in column (3) shows that the squared second factor, by contrast, appears to be driven entirely by statement surprises. The coefficient on STATEMENT SURPRISE is both highly statistically significant (t = 4.54) and

---

[23] We took all occasions when the policy bias or the balance of risks differed from the median survey responses as surprises.

Table 2. United States: Regressions of Squared Factors on Statement Dummy Variables

Independent variable	*Dependent variable*					
	Factor 1		Factor 2		Factor 3	
	(1)	(2)	(3)	(4)	(5)	(6)
Constant	64.7	64.7	24.1	24.1	3.2	3.2
	(1.85)	(1.82)	(1.48)	(1.51)	(1.10)	(1.10)
Statement	**131.6**	**131.6**	18.3	18.3	6.3	6.3
	(2.04)	(2.03)	(0.61)	(0.63)	(1.18)	(1.17)
Statement Surprise	**-149.4**	-139.5	**153.3**	**120.7**	8.1	7.9
	(-2.05)	(-1.75)	(4.54)	(3.35)	(1.33)	(1.19)
Path Surprise	--	-34.2	--	**112.5**	--	0.6
		(-0.32)		(2.31)		(0.07)
Adj. R-Squared	0.04	0.04	0.26	0.30	0.07	0.07

t-statistics are given in parentheses. Coefficients significant at the 5 percent level are highlighted in bold.

economically important; the regression implies that, on average, the variance of the second factor during the one-hour window surrounding the release of the statement is about 196 basis points when the statement is surprising but only about 42 basis points when the statement is as expected. Moreover, the variance of the second factor is not significantly different from zero on days when no statement is released or when the statement is as anticipated. This result suggests that "surprise" statements have a major impact on policy expectations a year ahead.

The magnitude of the third factor seems unrelated to policy statements, as neither dummy variable enters significantly into the regression for the square of that factor (column 5). In other words, we find no evidence that FOMC statements affect the five-year Treasury yield independent of their effect on year-ahead expectations. (However, recall from table 1 that independent variation in year-ahead policy expectations—the second factor—accounts for the bulk of the variance of the five-year Treasury yield during the periods surrounding FOMC decisions. Thus, holding the current policy decision constant, a surprising statement has an important effect on yields at the five-year horizon, albeit indirectly through its effects on one-year-ahead policy expectations.) As we saw above, the third factor is quite small and may simply reflect residual noise in the five-year yield.

Investors are most interested in statements that provide hints about the Committee's inclinations regarding future policy actions (as opposed to, for example, statements that describe past economic developments). From the Committee's point of view, the effects on market expectations of statements bearing on the future course of policy should also be of particular interest, since this is the type of statement that theory

41

suggests should be most useful when the policy rate is near the zero bound. To examine whether statements that provide new information about the likely future path of monetary policy are particularly influential, we used the sources noted above to identify nine statements among the 31 "surprise" statements that seemed most explicitly focused on the likely future path of policy. The dummy variable PATH SURPRISE takes a value of one on the dates of these statements.

A number of these statements occurred recently, in a period when the FOMC was attempting to provide additional stimulus for the economy despite the fact that the federal funds rate had already been reduced to a level as low as 100 basis points. For example, in August 2003, the FOMC stated that "policy accommodation can be maintained for a considerable period," marking the first time that the FOMC statement discussed an extended outlook for its policy path.[24] This phrase was repeated in FOMC statements following the September, October, and December meetings. At its January 2004 meeting, the FOMC replaced the "considerable period" phrase with the assertion that "the Committee believes that it can be patient in removing its policy accommodation." This substitution caused long-dated Treasury yields to jump 15 to 25 basis points, a clear indication that the Committee's language was important in shaping longer-term policy expectations. Policymaking by thesaurus continued through 2004. After repeating the "patient" language after its March meeting, the May FOMC statement replaced this phrase with a statement that it "believes that policy accommodation can be removed at a pace that is likely to be measured," and it maintained that assessment through the August meeting. These statements, because they are so explicitly focused on the policy path,

---

[24] The "policy bias" that was part of the statement for the brief period from May 1999 to December 1999 was usually interpreted as pertaining to a much shorter time frame, such as the inter-meeting period.

may provide the best natural experiments for assessing what could be accomplished at the zero bound.

As can be seen in columns 2, 4, and 6 of table 2, the PATH SURPRISE dummy enters significantly only in the regression explaining the square of the second factor, further confirming the association of this factor with policy statements. Relative to a situation in which an unsurprising statement is issued, a surprise statement about the likely future course of policy increases the variance of the second factor during the event window by 233 basis points (the sum of the coefficients on surprise statements and policy path statements), indicating that statements providing new information about the prospective path of policy have a powerful effect on year-ahead policy expectations and hence, indirectly, on the five-year Treasury yield as well.

So far we have shown that year-ahead policy expectations react strongly to unexpected changes in the statement, in the sense that the absolute change in year-ahead expectations tends to be much larger when the statement is unexpected. We have not yet shown that the change in expectations is in the predicted direction, e.g., that unexpectedly "hawkish" statements cause expectations to shift toward a greater degree of policy tightening. To take this additional step, while recognizing once again that the quantification of purely qualitative statements is necessarily hazardous, we used the source materials described earlier to "sign" the 31 surprise statements in terms of their apparent implications for subsequent monetary policy actions. We summarized this information in a dummy variable, SIGNED STATEMENT, assigned the value of +1 for surprise "hawkish" statements (those that implied a higher future path of the federal funds rate than expected), -1 for surprise "dovish" statements, and 0 for all other observations, including those with non-surprising statements or no statements at all. We then regressed the *levels* of each of the three factors on the signed dummy variable. We also tried regressing the levels of the factors on the signed values of statements corresponding to policy path surprises (SIGNED PATH, defined as the product of the SIGNED STATEMENT and PATH SURPRISE dummies.)

The results, shown in table 3, further strengthen our findings. Columns 1, 2, 5, and 6 of the table show that no significant relationship exists between the signed statement surprises and either the first or third factors. In contrast, signed surprises have a large and highly statistically significant effect on the second factor, with hawkish (dovish) statements pushing up (down) year-ahead policy expectations by 12 basis points, on average (column 3.) The effects are even larger (16 basis points) when we restrict our attention to the 9 policy path surprises (column 4). Recalling from table 1a that the loading of the five-year yield on the second factor is 0.64, we can also estimate that, the current policy surprise held constant, a surprisingly hawkish statement raises the five-year yield by about 8 basis points and a hawkish statement about the policy path raises the five-year yield by about 10 basis points.

[Table 3 about here]

Conditioning effects of policy statements

The immediate effects of official FOMC statements on policy expectations likely underestimate the overall impact of FOMC communications on expectations; for example, our focus on statements alone ignores the potential effects of speeches and testimony by FOMC members. Also, beyond their immediate effects, FOMC statements

Table 3. United States: Regressions of Factors (in Levels) on Signed Statement Dummy Variables

Independent variable	Dependent variable					
	Factor 1		Factor 2		Factor 3	
	(1)	(2)	(3)	(4)	(5)	(6)
Signed Statement Surprise	1.4 (0.83)	--	**11.5** (10.21)	--	-0.4 (-0.68)	--
Signed Path Surprise	--	-1.5 (-0.49)	--	**15.8** (6.38)	--	1.3 (1.37)
Adj. R-Squared	-0.03	-0.03	0.47	0.26	-0.02	-0.01

t-statistics in parentheses. Coefficients significant at the 5 percent level are in bold.

may affect the formation of policy expectations by influencing how those expectations respond to various sorts of incoming data. In particular, to the extent that FOMC policy commitments are conditional, that is, tied to specific economic developments, policy expectations should react more strongly to macroeconomic news that bears on those developments.

A leading example is the market's responsiveness to monthly reports on payroll employment.[25] Throughout the recent period, the Committee was concerned about the "jobless" nature of the recovery and repeatedly pointed to weakness in the labor market as a key factor shaping the outlook for policy. When the Chairman Greenspan introduced the phrase "considerable period" in his semi-annual report to Congress in July 2003, he indicated the Fed's concerns about resource utilization, and "unwelcome disinflation." (On several occasions in testimony, Greenspan has also indicated his preference for the payroll employment series over the household employment series as a measure of current conditions in the labor market.) Each FOMC statement that used the "considerable period" language also discussed labor market conditions, and the December 2003 statement tied the "considerable period" outlook for policy closely to "slack" in resource use. Statements since December 2003 have continued both to place substantial weight on labor market conditions (as well as inflation) and to provide information about the Committee's policy expectations.

With this background, if FOMC communication is effective, one might expect to find that financial markets have become more sensitive to news about payroll employment. Figure 2 confirms this hypothesis. The figure shows the responsiveness,

---

[25] A second important example, not pursued here for reasons of space, is the responsiveness of the market to data on core inflation.

45

over a 30-minute window, of the ten-year Treasury yield to surprises in monthly payrolls, where the surprise is defined as the reported payroll number less the median survey expectation as provided by Money Market Services. The sample is divided into the period through August 2003, the release just prior to the meeting when the "considerable period" language was introduced, and the period from September 2003 to the present. In the earlier period, as indicated by the thin regression line, a positive surprise of 100,000 payroll jobs translated into a 4-basis-point increase in ten-year Treasury yields during the 30-minute window. Since September 2003, this responsiveness has strengthened, as is visible from the larger data points. The regression line for the recent sub-sample shows that ten-year Treasury yields increased 11 basis points for every surprise of 100,000 jobs above the consensus expectation. The difference in coefficients is statistically significant.

If FOMC communications are responsible for the increased responsiveness of yields (and the associated policy expectations) to unexpected changes in payroll employment, it should also be the case that markets have responded less to macroeconomic developments not flagged by the Committee as likely to have a strong bearing on policy decisions. This especially the case over the period when, conditioned on the ongoing sluggishness of hiring, the Committee had indicated that policy would remain highly accommodative. That this latter conjecture is likely to be true is shown by figure 3, which reports implied volatility measures derived from options on Eurodollar futures. These measures are market-based estimates of the expected volatility of the three-month interest rate over two horizons: four months and one year. As can be seen in the figure, the short-horizon volatility measure fell to historic lows during the second half of 2003. The same result does not hold at the longer horizon. These data provide a bit of evidence that the FOMC's communications in the second half of 2003 reduced the volatility of ("anchored") near-term policy expectations. As we have seen that policy expectations simultaneously became more sensitive to certain types of macroeconomic news, such as the payroll report, the decline in overall volatility suggests that the responsiveness of markets to other types of news declined.

[Figure 2 about here]

[Figure 3 about here]

Shaping Policy Expectations: Evidence from a Macro-Finance Model of the Term Structure

Our event studies confirm that FOMC statements have important influences, both direct and indirect, on private sector policy expectations. Event studies have the drawback, however, of showing only very short-term effects. They may overstate the more important longer-term effects, if for example yields tend to over-react in the period just around announcements; or they may understate the longer-term effects, by not accounting for types of communication other than statements, for example. In this section we address this issue by developing a benchmark "macro-finance" model of the term structure. Here and in additional exercises in the remainder of the paper, our model provides estimates of what the term structure would have been, given the state of the economy and the stance of monetary policy, but excluding other factors. By comparing this benchmark estimate of the term structure with the actual term structure at crucial junctures, we may be able to get a sense of the quantitative impacts of these other factors on the maturity structure of interest rates.

Figure 2. The response of Treasury yields to the employment report

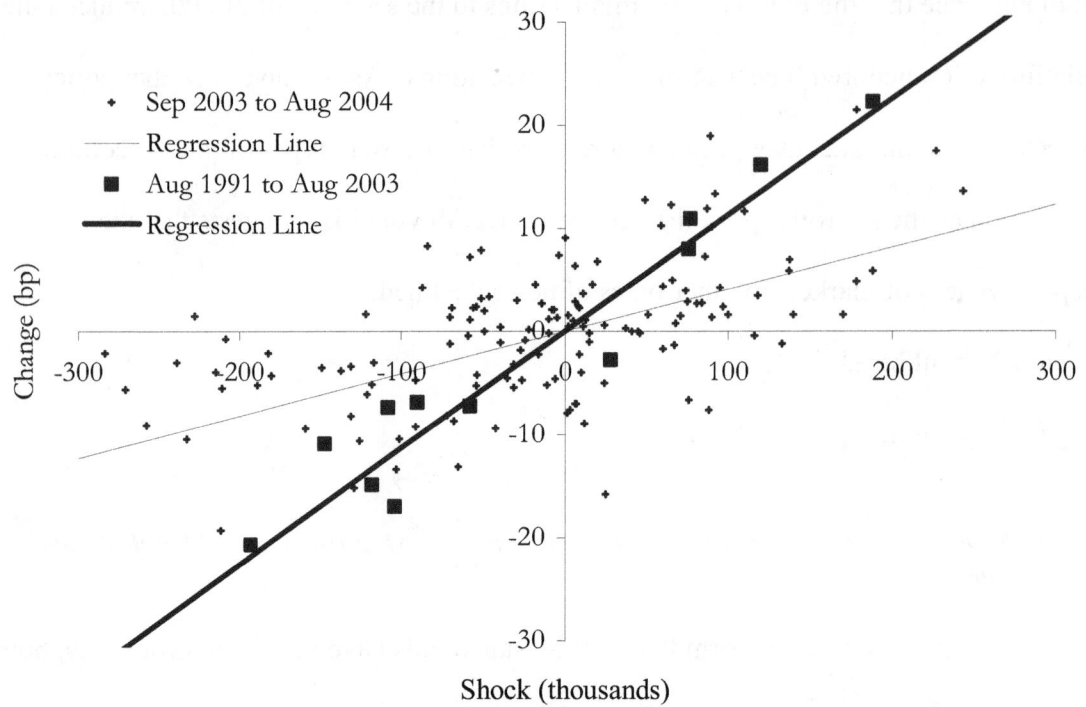

The change in the Treasury yield from 8:25 to 8:55 on the days of employment reports. Regression lines are estimated over the two subsamples listed. The graph cuts off a couple of very large surprises, such as the 408,000-job surprise in March 1996, but those observations are included in the regression estimation.

Figure 3. The Implied Volatility of Short-term Interest Rates
Annualized rate, expressed in percentage points

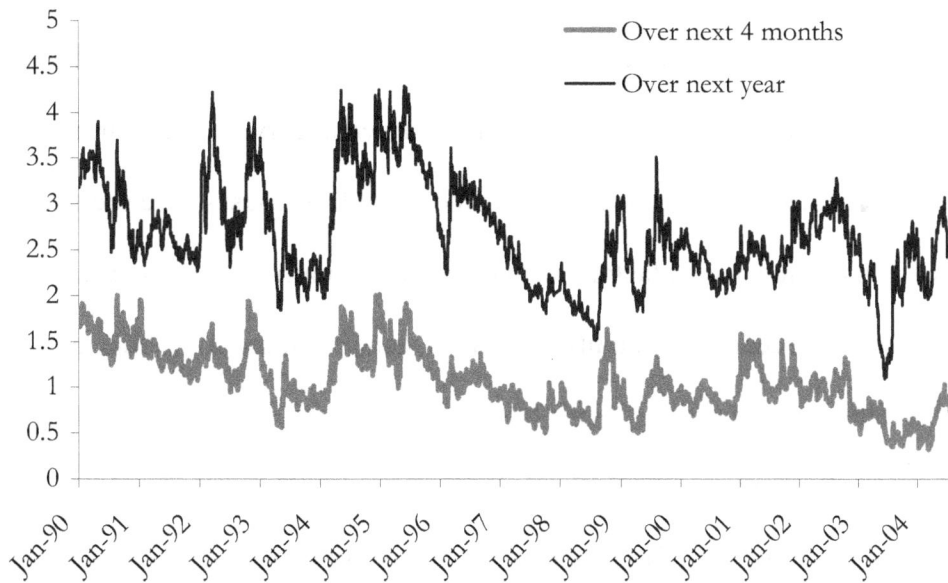

The figure shows the width of a 90% confidence interval for the federal funds rate over the horizon shown. These measures are derived from the implied volatility of the three-month Eurodollar rate from options on Eurodollar futures.

m_{t+1} is the one-period pricing kernel. Because we will be considering zero-coupon bonds, the payout from the bonds is simply their value in the following period, so that the following recursive relationship holds:

$$(2) \qquad P_t^n = E_t[m_{t+1} P_{t+1}^{n-1}]$$

where n is the remaining life of the bond and the terminal value of the bond, P_{t+n}^0, is normalized to equal 1.

Following the approach of Ang and Piazzesi (2003) and Ang, Piazzesi, and Wei (2004), we assume that the pricing kernel is conditionally log-normal, as follows:

$$(3) \qquad m_{t+1} = \exp\left(-y_t^{(1)} - \frac{1}{2}\lambda_t'\lambda_t - \lambda_t'\varepsilon_{t+1}\right),$$

where the λ_t are the market prices of risk associated with the VAR innovations (the source of uncertainty in the mode), and $y_t^{(1)}$ is the one-period interest rate expressed on a continuously-compounded basis. As already noted, we assume that the prices of risk are linear in the state variables:

$$(4) \qquad \lambda_t = \lambda_0 + \lambda_1 X_t.$$

We restrict the prices of risk to be zero for all but the first five elements of λ_t corresponding to the independent factors in the VAR—that is, we assume that the prices of risk λ_t depend only on the contemporaneous values of the VAR. (Recall that the final fifteen elements of the stacked column vector X_t are lags of the five factors.) These assumptions imply that only 30 parameters must be estimated in this block of the

50

model, a manageable number, while still allowing the model the flexibility needed to provide a good empirical fit of the term structure data.

Manipulation of equations (1)-(3) shows that the zero-coupon yields can be written as linear functions of the state variables, as follows:

$$(5) \qquad\qquad y_t^{(n)} = a_n + b_n' X_t,$$

where $a_n = -A_n / n$ and $b_n = -B_n / n$, and the vector A_n and the matrix B_n are determined by the following recursive formulas:

$$(6) \qquad A_{n+1} = A_n + B_n'(\mu - \Sigma\lambda_0) + \frac{1}{2} B_n' \Sigma\Sigma' B_n - \delta_0$$

$$(7) \qquad\qquad B_{n+1} = (\Phi - \Sigma\lambda_1)B_n - \delta_1,$$

The starting values for these equations are $A_1 = \delta_0$ and $B_1 = \delta_1$, and the parameters δ_0 and δ_1 describe the relationship of the one-period yield to the state vector, that is, $y_t^{(1)} = \delta_0 + \delta_1 X_t$. In our application, as the one-period yield (the federal funds rate) is included in the state variable, this relationship is trivial: All elements of δ_0 and δ_1 are zero except for the element of δ_1 that picks out the current value of the funds rate, which is set to unity.

Given a set of prices of risk, the entire Treasury yield curve can be derived using equation (5). We estimate the prices of risk by minimizing the sum of squared prediction errors for zero-coupon Treasury yields at maturities of six months and one, two, three, four, five, seven, and ten years. Our data are zero-coupon Treasury yields, based on the

Fisher-Nychka-Zervos (1995) yield curve for the period 1982 to 1987 and on the zero-coupon yield curve constructed at the Board of Governors for the period since 1987.

Our model contributes to the growing literature including macroeconomic variables into no-arbitrage term structure models. An appealing feature of our framework is the substantial simplification in estimation and analysis achieved by our assumption that all the factors driving the term structure are observable economic and monetary variables. As noted earlier, related models, such as those of Ang and Piazzesi (2003) and Rudebusch and Wu (2003), typically include unobserved factors as determinants of the term structure and even of the observed economic variables in the system. The use of unobserved factors has advantages in some applications, but it greatly complicates estimation and may make the economic interpretation of the results more difficult.[28] Our approach instead directly links the term structure, observable economic conditions the providing us with a benchmark for gauging the potential effects of unusual monetary policy strategies.

[Figure 4 about here.]

Estimation of the model explains the term structure over time. Figure 4 compares the fitted and actual time series for the two-year and ten-year Treasury yields. The model predicts Treasury yields reasonably well at all maturities: As reported in the first column of Table 4, The standard deviation of the model's prediction error equals 34 basis points at the six-month maturity and increases to around 80 basis points for longer maturities. Also shown in figure 4 are the two-year and ten-year "risk-neutral" yields. These are

---

[28] Ang, Piazzesi, and Wei (2003) employ a model in which, as in our analysis, the pricing kernel is assumed to be a function of observable variables. However, the only macroeconomic variable in their model is GDP growth, and they do not focus on the properties of the term structure model itself but on the implications of their framework for predicting GDP growth.

Figure 4. Actual and predicted Treasury yields
percent

Two-year Treasury Yield

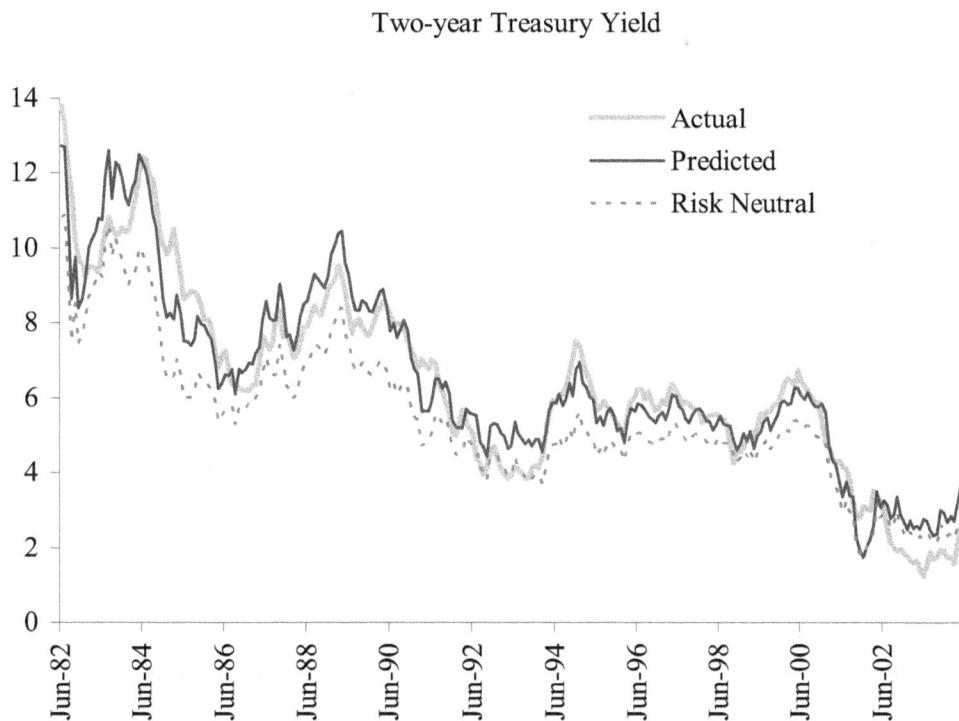

Ten-year Treasury Yield

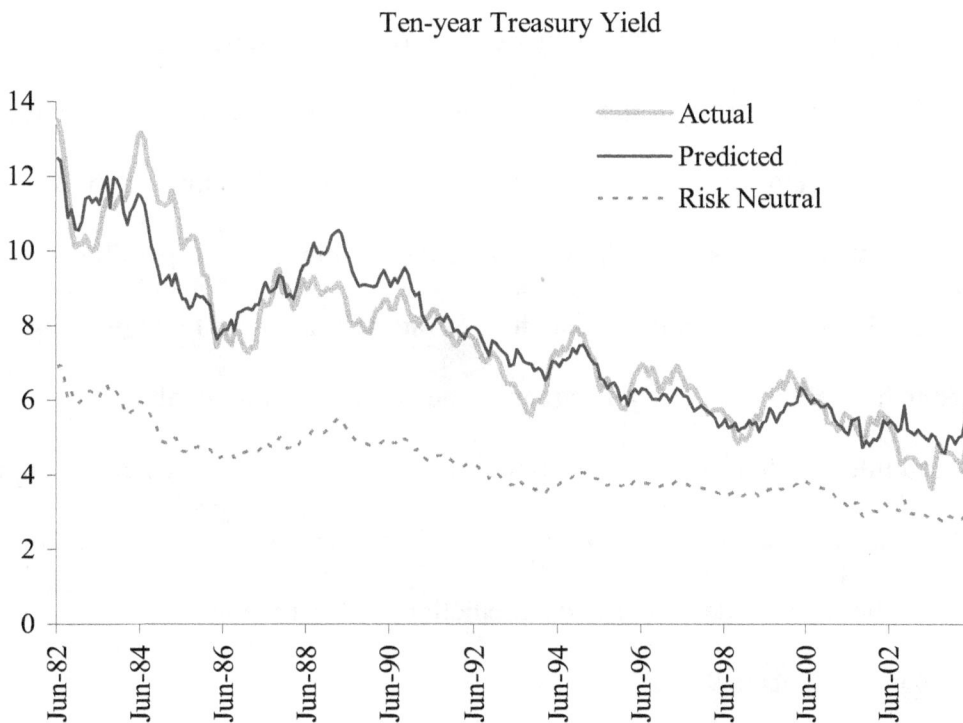

derived by setting the prices of risk equal to zero—that is, they are the rates that investors would demand if they were risk neutral. The difference between these lines and the predicted yields, then, are estimated risk premiums. Figure 4 shows that estimated risk premiums for longer-dated securities have declined over time, presumably reflecting greater stability in the economy and in policy, but they remain fairly large. Of particular note is that variations in the risk premium are estimated to account for a significant portion of the variation in long-term yields.

In the event-study analysis described earlier, we found that an important part of the effect of a monetary policy decisions is transmitted through its impact on year-ahead policy expectations, which in turn depend importantly on FOMC statements. Those changes in year-ahead policy expectations, as captured by the Eurodollar futures rate, were found to be important for determining longer-term yields (the five-year yield, in our analysis).

The importance of year-ahead policy expectations for longer-dated yields is generally confirmed by our term-structure fitting exercise. We can assess the importance of innovations of the future rate by ordering it last in a Cholesky decomposition. In doing so, we are attributing as much of the movements in future rates as possible to the other variables. Even so, innovations to the futures rate are important for explaining movements in the yield curve. As can be seen in the second column of table 4, excluding the year-ahead futures rate innovations from the VAR causes significant deterioration in the fit of the estimated model, particularly at shorter horizons (table 4). For example, doing so raises the standard deviation of the prediction error for the two-year Treasury yield from 74 basis points to 98 basis points.

[Table 4 about here]

One is tempted to combine the result of the event study (that FOMC statements have a substantial influence on year-ahead policy expectations) with the result from the term-structure fitting exercise (that year-ahead policy expectations are important determinants of Treasury yields) to conclude that FOMC statements have an important influence on the term structure. That conclusion may be a bit premature. Notably, the innovations to the Eurodollar futures rate obtained from the VAR need not correspond closely to the innovations to the same variable obtained from the high-frequency event study. To illustrate this point, table 5 compares, for various sub-samples, the monthly standard deviation of innovations to the year-ahead Eurodollar futures rate, as calculated from the VAR (left column) and by summing the changes in the Eurodollar rate around FOMC decisions (right column).[29] In general, the variance of the VAR innovations to the Eurodollar rate is significantly greater than the variance to the Eurodollar rate directly associated with FOMC decisions. Several plausible explanations for this difference come to mind: First, the movements of the Eurodollar rate in the hour around FOMC decisions certainly do not capture all of the effects of FOMC communications, including the effects of speeches and testimonies and the point, demonstrated earlier, that FOMC statements can affect the responsiveness of policy expectations to various kinds of macroeconomic news. Indeed, as table 5 illustrates, as the FOMC has made greater use of communications strategies, particularly since mid-2003, the variation of the Eurodollar rate around FOMC decisions has risen, while the variation in the corresponding VAR innovation actually fell, possibly reflecting better anchoring of short-term policy

---

[29] Table 4 begins in July 1991, corresponding to the earliest date covered by our event study. Break dates in the sample include the date at which the FOMC began announcing interest-rate decisions (February 1994) and the date at which the FOMC adopted the "considerable period" language (August 2003).

Table 4. Prediction Errors for Treasury Yields
Standard deviation, in basis points

Maturity	VAR with ED Shocks	VAR w/o ED Shocks
6 months	33.6	62.8
1 year	50.7	79.4
2 years	73.9	98.2
3 years	81.5	101.1
4 years	82.2	98.3
5 years	80.1	94.2
7 years	81.0	92.2
10 years	78.7	87.0

expectations. That said, it seems clear that not all of the VAR innovation represents unmeasured communications effects; certainly, some part of the VAR innovations to the Eurodollar futures rate surely reflects responses of policy expectations to developments in the economy unrelated to FOMC communications (and not captured by the economic variables included in the VAR).

[Table 5 about here]

As a simple case study, we considered in more detail the VAR innovations and the event-study innovations during the period in which the FOMC introduced the "considerable period" language, August 2003 to December 2003. During that period, according to the event study, FOMC communications pushed down the Eurodollar futures rate by a cumulative 19 basis points, whereas the VAR shocks lowered the future rate by 63 basis points.[30] As an upper bound on the effect of "considerable period" on the term structure, figure 5 uses our estimated model of the term structure to show the effect on the yield curve associated with a 63-basis-point decline in the Eurodollar futures rate. The model predicts an effect of "considerable period" ranging from about 20 basis points at the two-year horizon to about 7 basis points at the ten-year horizon. Of course, if the cumulative effect were only 19 basis points, the impact on the term structure shown in figure 5 would be something less than half as large. As with all empirical work, the truth may lie in between.

[Figure 5 about here]

Overall, the evidence suggests that FOMC statements have importantly shaped the policy expectations of investors, particularly over the past five years. Indeed, yield

---

[30] Because the VAR models month-average variables, we sum the realization through January, as the removal of the "considerable period" language did not take place until the end of the month.

Table 5. Magnitude of Year-Ahead-Futures Shocks
Standard deviations, in basis points

Sample	VAR Shock	Event-study Shock
7/91 to 1/94	35.9	4.2
2/94 to 4/99	35.2	6.8
5/99 to 7/03	40.1	8.2
8/03 to 5/04	25.2	11.7

The event-study shock is aggregated to a monthly variable to be comparable to the VAR shock.

Figure 5. Effects of futures rate shocks during the "considerable period" episode
Change in Treasury yields, percentage points

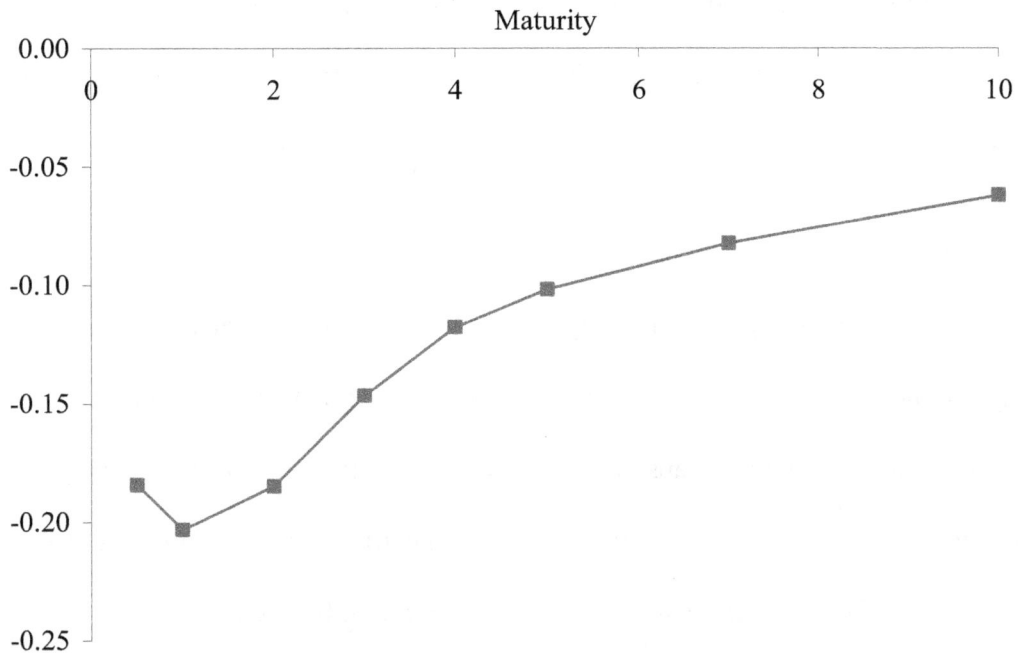

The cumulative shift in Treasury yields predicted by the futures rate shocks from the VAR realized from August 2003 to December 2003.

curve movements around FOMC decisions cannot be adequately described by the unexpected component of policy decisions, but are instead influenced to a greater extent by a second factor which appears to be associated with surprises in the policy statements. These findings suggest that policymakers may have some scope for influencing investors' expectations if the federal funds rate were to fall to the zero bound.

The effects of changing the supply of assets

We turn now to evidence bearing on the third type of non-conventional policy, changes in the composition of the central bank's balance sheet or targeted asset purchases. The question to be answered is whether substitution among assets is sufficiently imperfect so that large purchases of a specific class of asset might affect its yield, over and above any influence those purchases might have on investors' expectations about the future course of the short-term interest rate. Of course, the Federal Reserve has not undertaken any such actions in recent years. However, it still may be possible to learn about the effects of such actions by looking at the effects on yields of other actual or expected changes in the relative supplies of assets.

We identified three episodes in the past five years in which market participants in the United States came to anticipate significant changes in the relative supplies of Treasury securities. The "natural experiments" we consider are (1) the Treasury's announcement in 1999 of a plan to buy back government debt in the face of prospective budget surpluses; (2) the investment in Treasury securities of foreign-exchange-market intervention proceeds by Asian official institutions; and (3) the conviction on the part of some financial-market participants in the summer of 2003 that the Federal Reserve might resort to targeted purchases of long-term Treasury securities in order to combat incipient deflation.

We look at each episode through two prisms. First, we first consider the movement in a number of yields in narrow windows surrounding important announcements—in essence, relying on an event-study methodology to isolate the market response to news. Then we apply our no-arbitrage model of the U.S. term structure to provide a benchmark estimate of the pattern of yields, attributing residual movements to relative supply effects.

(1) *The paydown of Treasury bonds.* We begin with "the case of the disappearing Treasury bonds," the debt buyback episode of 1999. In the mid-1990s, rapidly rising real incomes and expanding equity values increased both the tax base and the effective tax rate in the United States. The swelling of Treasury tax coffers, combined with some discipline in spending, turned budgetary deficits into surpluses. By the end of the decade, extrapolation of those trends led to forecasts that Treasury debt would disappear in a decade.[31] The Treasury dealt with those windfalls in three stages. Initially, it cut bill issuance as the deficit shrank, which reportedly led to some deterioration of the liquidity in that segment of the market and a shift toward three-month Eurodollar instruments as the hedging vehicles of choice. Next, the Treasury trimmed issuance of longer-term securities by eliminating a few maturities and scaling back the volume of the remainder. Third, the Treasury announced in August 1999 that it was considering buying back some older, off-the-run issues, so that its remaining auctions would remain sizable enough to retain investors' interest.

---

[31] Reinhart and Sack (2000) review the economic consequences of such an outcome. Auerbach and Gale (2000) provided a real-time reminder of the fickleness of far-ahead fiscal forecasts.

Two events stand out as marking a significant shift in investors' view of the prospects for issuance—the midquarter refunding announcements of February 2000 and November 2001. At the 2000 refunding, the undersecretary for domestic finance, Gary Gensler, made a comment suggesting that the ten-year note would replace the thirty-year bond as the benchmark long-term security, triggering speculation that the issuance of thirty-year bonds would be discontinued. Indeed, the Treasury confirmed at the November 2001 refunding announcement that it would stop selling the long bond.

Actual market repurchases began in March 2000 and cumulated to $67 billion when ended to 2002. Only bonds were purchased, the bulk of which matured beyond 2015. These debt buybacks represented a significant relative supply shock, as they were concentrated in one maturity segment and amounted to about one-tenth of the outstanding stock of bonds (as of the beginning of 2000). Moreover, they were widely expected to be much larger than they were, with some dealers in early 2000 estimating that the size of buybacks would reach $100 billion per year soon thereafter. Thus, in terms of anticipated supply the shock was much larger.

Views about the magnitude of debt buybacks seem to evolve over time and thus do not lend themselves easily to event study analysis. However, we can look at the immediate market impact of the two quarterly refunding announcements that provided information about the discontinuation of bond issuance (February 2000 and November 2001). There is little reason to suspect that either announcement should have influenced the market outlook for net issuance of government debt. Rather, the news bore exclusively on the pattern of security sales. Even so, as shown in table 6, the Treasury yield curve rotated down dramatically in both cases when investors learnt that the managers of the government debt would shy away from longer-maturity securities.

[Table 6 about here]

The market's reaction is seen more starkly in the movement in yields across the maturity spectrum in the month bracketing the February announcement, as plotted in figure 6. No doubt, macroeconomic news relevant to interest-rate expectations and risk attitudes and perceptions also came out during that month. But the fact that yields on bonds as opposed to notes declined sharply over a month in which important information about the elimination of the issuance of long-term securities was released seems suggestive of the possibility that relative supplies matter.

[Figure 6 about here]

We can also look at this episode using our estimated term-structure model to control for variations in the economy and monetary policy over the period surrounding the buyback news. Figure 7 shows the prediction error of the model for the twenty-year Treasury yield in the period around the debt buyback. We see that yields during this period dropped about 100 basis points below what is predicted by the model. This is a significant deviation in economic terms, although errors of this size are not unusual as indicated earlier in Table 4. [Figure 7 about here]

These results are only suggestive, of course, in that the term-structure model is unlikely to capture all the determinants of yields or control adequately for shifts in expectations. In addition, the precise magnitude of the effects is not clear, in that the size of the shock is hard to determine as we do not know the probability that investors were attaching to a sizable paydown. Moreover, we cannot be sure that the effects shown here

Table 6. Changes in Treasury yields around announcements of bond supply

basis points

Maturity	February 2000 Quarterly Refunding	November 2001 Quarterly Refunding
2 years	-5	1
5 years	-13	-9
10 years	-13	-20
30 years	-27	-43

Changes in the yields of the on-the-run issues from the day before the announcement to the day after.

Figure 6. Treasury yields around the announcement of the debt buyback program
Percent

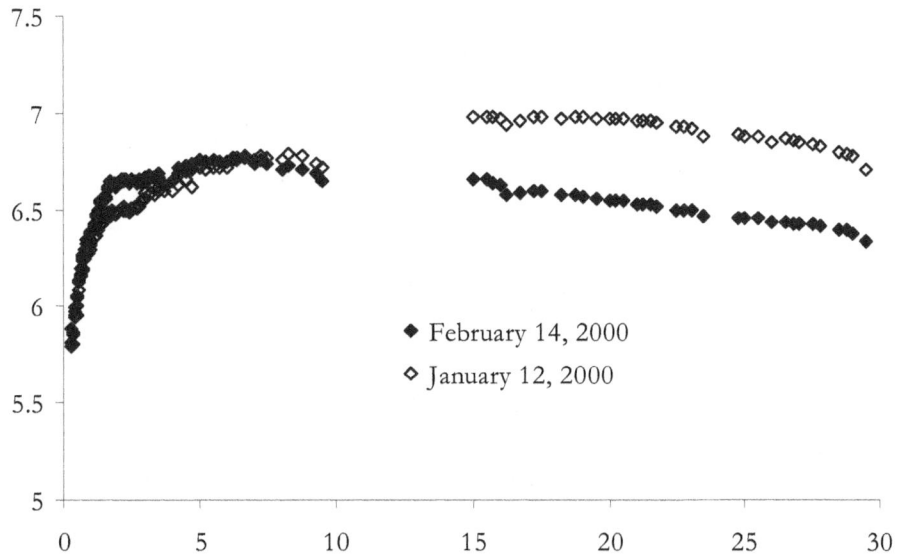

The yields on all outstanding Treasury notes and bonds, excluding callable issues.

Figure 7. Prediction errors from the macro-term structure model
Basis points

Twenty-year Treasury Yield

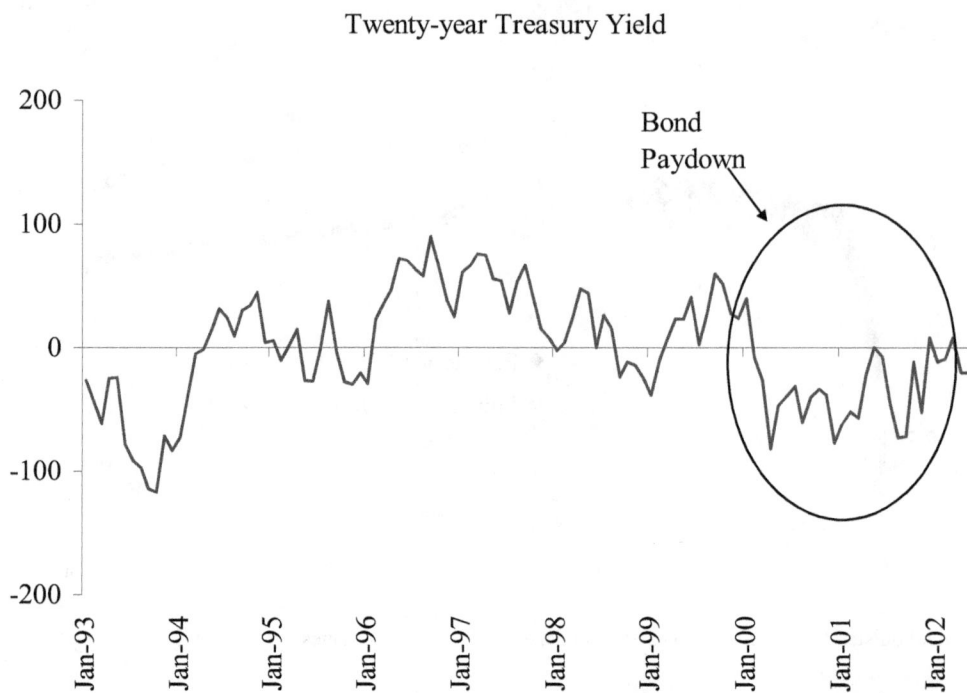

are "scalable" in a predictable manner, so these results give little quantitative information to policymakers contemplating targeted asset purchases. Finally, as we discussed earlier, movements in Treasury yields arising from targeted purchases need not pass through to the private rates that presumably influence spending decisions. As a bit of evidence on this last point, swap spreads—a good indicator of risk premiums on private securities— widened noticeably at the thirty-year maturity (but not at the two-year maturity) during the period that long-dated Treasury yields declined (figure 8). The sharp increase in long-term swap spreads and its subsequent unwinding coincides closely with the dip in predictor errors in figure 7. Thus, private rates apparently did not follow the long end of the Treasury curve down as investor concerns regarding the availability of certain maturity classes of Treasuries mounted.

[Figure 8 about here]

(2) Purchases of U.S. Treasury securities by foreign official institutions. In the wake of the Asian currency crisis in 1998, policymakers in the many Asian economies apparently decided that it was desirable to limit fluctuations of their currencies against the value of the dollar. The result has been a steadily accumulation of dollar reserves, often in the form of Treasury securities. For instance, securities held in custody at the Federal Reserve Bank of New York on the behalf of foreign official institutions now total about $1-1/4 trillion, about double the amount at the end of 1998. Japanese authorities, in particular, intervened heavily in foreign exchange markets from 2003 to the first quarter of 2004 in an effort to counter or slow the yen's appreciation against the dollar. Japanese intervention purchases totaled $177 billion in 2003 and $138 billion in the first quarter of

Figure 8. Swap spreads during the paydown of Treasury bonds
Basis points

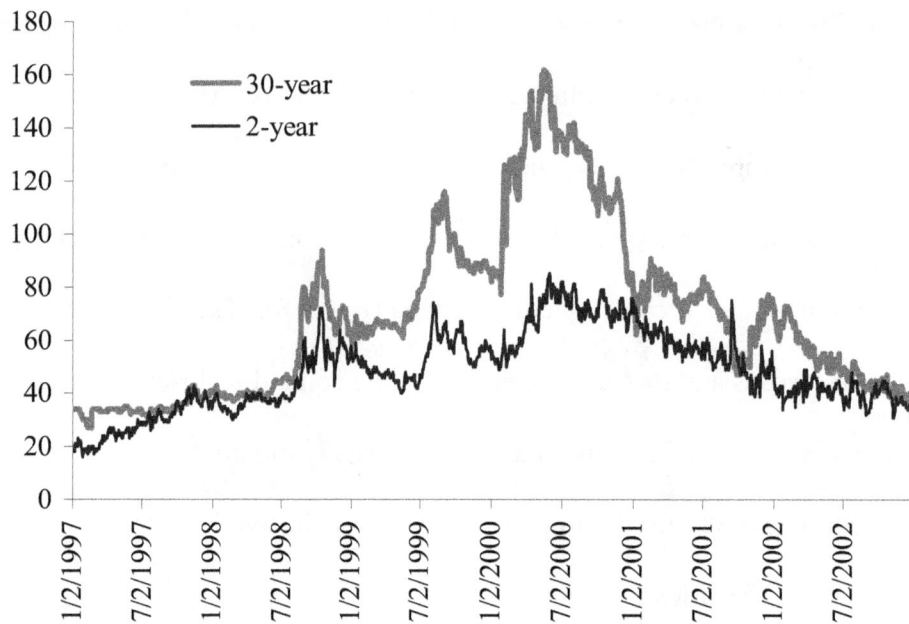

2004. The Japanese Ministry of Finance (MOF) holds the proceeds of intervention activities as either bank deposits or Treasury securities, and its deposit holdings generally are re-invested in Treasuries over time. The Japanese interventions in the five quarters ending in 2004:Q1 cumulated to about $300 billion that bond market participants anticipated would be invested in Treasury securities. Since the Japanese interventions were presumably only weakly linked at best to expectations about future U.S. monetary policy, these purchases provide the basis for a second natural experiment for testing the relationship between relative asset supplies and yields.

The simplest exercise is to regress the change in various Treasury yields to the volume dollar of intervention. While the interventions were not publicly announced, an examination of newspaper articles indicates that operations were immediately recognized by market participants, who appeared also generally to have an accurate understanding of the scale as well. Thus, even though foreign exchange market transactions settle at day $t+2$, the effects on Treasury yields should occur at date t as market participants anticipated near-term purchases of Treasury securities. However, to allow for the possibility that the market did not recognize the intervention until the settlement of the transaction, we looked at changes in yields from day $t-1$ to day $t+2$. The sample includes all Japanese interventions from January 3, 2000, to March 3, 2004. The regression results are shown in table 7. As can be seen in the left-hand column of the table, two-, five-, and ten-year Treasury yields all fell significantly on dates around Japanese interventions, and the estimated coefficients are highly statistically significant. Treasury bill yields did not react to interventions, perhaps because they are pinned down by the current and near-term expected path of the federal funds rate.

[Table 7 about here]

While these results are suggestive of an important role for relative asset supplies in the determination of yields, they suffer from potential problems of joint endogeneity. For example, weak economic data could cause Treasury yields to fall and the dollar to weaken, with the latter prompting foreign exchange intervention by the MOF. To try to address this problem, we excluded from the sample all days with major U.S. data releases (see notes to table), which produced smaller and less statistically significant coefficients, but the results remain broadly unchanged.

This episode provides us another opportunity to apply the no-arbitrage term-structure model to control for a changing macroeconomic environment. The results, shown in figure 9, indicate that both five-year and ten-year Treasury yields remained below the model's predictions by an average of 50 to 100 basis points over this period. This suggests that some force not captured in the model was exerting downward pressure on yields over this period. But while the evidence is suggestive of effects from MOF purchases, it is not conclusive. Indeed, yields moved down to those levels in advance of the sizable MOF intervention (but of course did not move back). Moreover, as indicated earlier in Table 4, prediction errors of this magnitude are not uncommon.

[Figure 9 about here]

(3) The 2003 deflation scare. From the fall of 2002 through the summer of 2003,

Table 7. Effects of Japanese Foreign Exchange Intervention on Treasury Yields

Basis point response to $1 billion intervention

Maturity	All Days	Excluding Days of Major U.S. Data Releases
3 months	-0.18 (1.16)	-0.18 (0.80)
2 years	**-0.78** (3.00)	-0.55 (1.99)
5 years	**-0.83** (2.37)	-0.66 (1.98)
10 years	**-0.73** (2.29)	**-0.66** (2.14)
Memo: Number of observations	1086	892
Memo: Number of interventions	140	112

The table reports coefficients from a regression of the change in the yield of the on-the-run issue from the day before the intervention to the day it settles (two days later) on the size of the intervention. Absolute t-statistics shown in parentheses, where standard errors are adjusted for autocorrelation and heteroskedasticity using the approach of Hodrick (1992). The second column excludes days on which there was the release of an employment report, GDP, ISM, retail sales, or consumer confidence.

Figure 9. Prediction Errors from the No-arbitrage VAR Model
Basis points

Five-year Treasury Yield

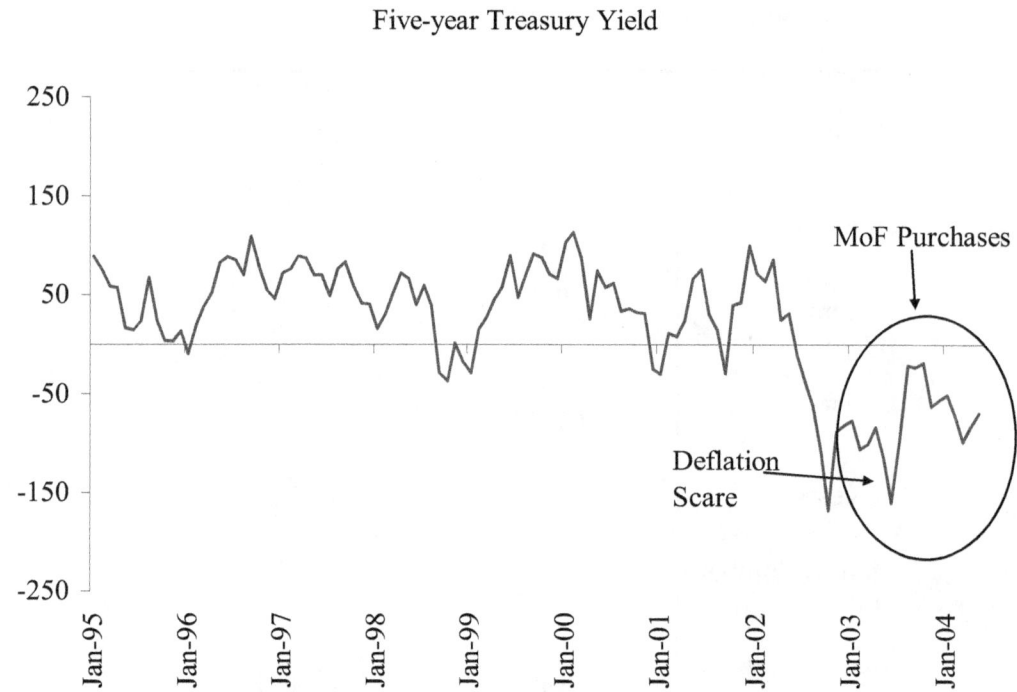

Ten-year Treasury Yield

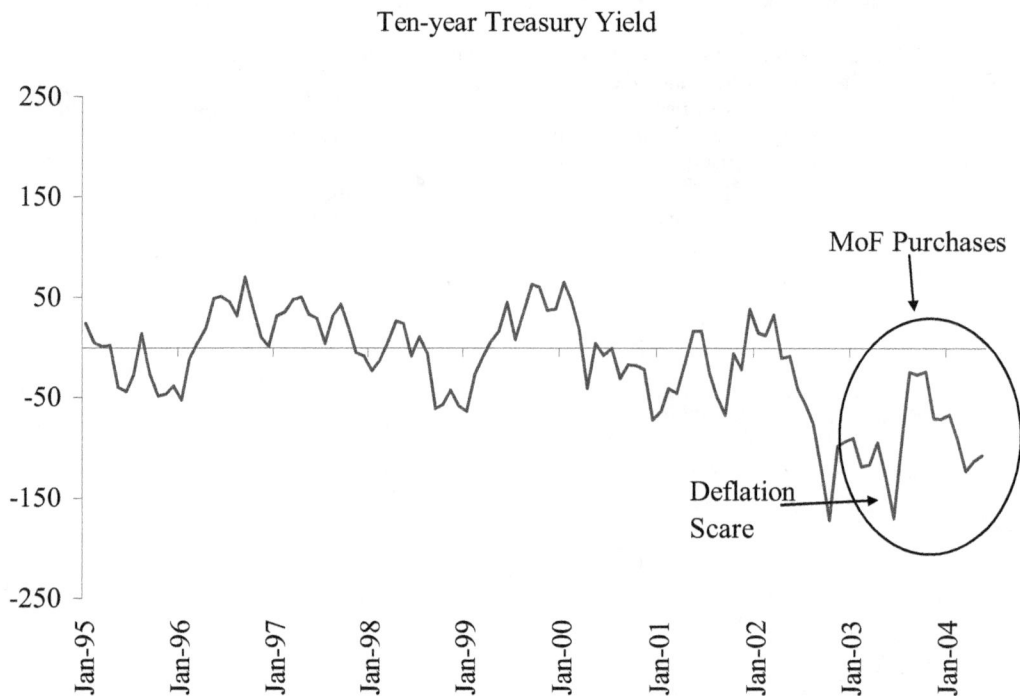

with the economy remaining weak, inflation low and apparently falling, and the federal

funds rate quite low, FOMC members began to talk about the risks of deflation in the

United States and the possible responses of monetary policy if the federal funds rate were

to hit its lower bound. A brief chronology of relevant speeches and testimonies by

Federal Reserve officials is provided in Table 8.

Although Federal Reserve officials consistently referred to the risk of deflation as

"remote" and the Committee's planning for the contingency of the ZLB to be purely

precautionary in nature, some market participants apparently interpreted these and other

public comments as indicating that the Federal Reserve was seriously considering

"unconventional" policy measures—in particular, purchasing large amounts of

longer-term Treasuries (probably ten-year notes). The perceived likelihood of such

actions seemed to peak after the May FOMC meeting, when the Committee pointed to

the (remote) risk of a substantial decline in inflation. The possibility of direct purchases

of ten-year notes was seen to be "taken off the table" when the June FOMC statement did

not mention it and when the Chairman testified to Congress in July that "situations

requiring special policy actions are most unlikely to arise." Again, large movements in

Treasury yields were observed on many of those days, with little alternative explanation.

Most notably, the ten-year Treasury yield fell sharply on the May FOMC statement (20

basis points) and the Chairman's speech in early June (10 basis points), and then rose

abruptly following the June FOMC statement (26 basis points) and the Chairman's

testimony in July (20 basis points).

Of course, the FOMC never undertook targeted purchases of Treasury securities,

but in an efficient market even the (incorrect) anticipation of such an event should affect yields. Figure 9 above shows a sharp downward spike in the model errors in May and June 2003, which is reversed in July. These findings, taken at face value, suggest that the perceived possibility of Treasury purchases had an impact on the order of 50 basis points or more. Once again, we must be particulary vary of identification issues. The events that conveyed information about the possibility of Federal Reserve purchases of Treasuries most likely also conveyed information to the public about the risk of deflation. Changes in the perceived risk of deflation would affect long-term yields independent of supply effects. Nonetheless, it is interesting to note that the downward spike in figure 9 stands out the most for the ten-year Treasury yield—the security that was perceived to be the most likely candidate for Federal Reserve purchases.

[Table 8 about here]

If the Federal Reserve were willing to purchase an unlimited amount of a particular asset, say a Treasury security, at a fixed price, there is little doubt that it could establish that asset's price. Presumably, this would be true even if the Federal Reserve's commitment to purchase the long-lived asset was promised for a future date.

Conceptually, it is useful to think of the Federal Reserve as providing investors in that security with a put option allowing them to sell back their holdings to the central bank at an established price. We can use our term-structure model to price that option. As a purely illustrative example, suppose the Federal Reserve announces its willingness to purchase the current ten-year (zero-coupon) Treasury security in one year at a yield of 5-1/2 percent. We will consider the value of this option jumping off from the last observation used in estimating our model, May 2004. (We assume that the rate in May 2004 equals the value predicted by our model, rather than the actual rate prevailing in that

Table 8. Notable events in the 2003 deflation scare

Date	Event	Content	Change 2-year Yield	Change 10-year yield
11/21/02	Bernanke speech	Presents arguments for making sure "it" doesn't happen here.	--	--
12/19/02	Greenspan speech	U.S. is nowhere close to sliding into a "pernicious" deflation	--	--
3/30/03	Reinhart speech	Discusses policy options at the zero bound	--	--
5/6/03	FOMC statement	Points to risk of an "unwelcome substantial fall in inflation"	-9	-20
5/22/03	Greenspan testimony	Deflation is a "serious" issue but the risks are "minor"	--	--
5/30/03	Reinhart speech	Emphasizes importance of shaping expectations	--	--
6/3/03	Greenspan speech	Mention of continued risk of declining inflation, need for a "firebreak"	-13	-10
6/25/03	FOMC ease, statement	Smaller-than-expected easing; statement does not mention unconventional policy measures	+29	+26
7/18/03	Chairman testimony	"Situations requiring special policy actions are most unlikely to arise"	+9	+20
7/23/03	Bernanke speech	FOMC should be willing to cut the funds rate to zero if necessary	--	--
8/12/03	FOMC statement	Drops "substantial" from risk of "unwelcome fall in inflation"	--	--

Table lists changes in the on-the-run Treasury yields that were strongly associated with the event listed. The changes listed for 5/6/03 and 6/25/03 are two-day changes, since the market continued to respond the day after the FOMC meeting.

month.) Without this commitment, according to our model, the yield on that security

would be expected to be 5.67 percent in a year, imply that the put option has a 58 percent

chance of ending up in the money. (The yield is given by $y_{t+12}^{(9)} = a_9 + b_9 X_{t+12}$.) The

strike price of the option will be $K = \exp(-9 * cap)$, where in our example $cap = .055$.

The price of the put option is

(8) $$put = E_t \left[m_{t+1} m_{t+2} m_{t+3} ... m_{t+12} (K - \exp(-a_9 - b_9 X_{t+12}))^+ \right].$$

We can compute this expectation by doing 10,000 simulations of the model. Note that

the simulations determine the correlation between the payout on the option and the value

that risk-averse investors place on those payouts (which depends on the evolution of the

state variables on the path to the payout). The results indicate that this option would

lower today's ten-year rate by 34 basis points. Note that this is more than the 17 basis

points that the option is "in the money," because the convexity of the option gives it

value.

Thinking of a pegging strategy in terms of options also highlights the potential

that the pass-through to private securities of such a strategy might be limited. In this

case, those investors holding a 10-year Treasury security receive the put option, but the

holder of (say) a 10-year high-grade corporate bond does not. Hence one would not

expect the value of the put option to be fully reflected in the price of the corporate bond.

Japan: A Modern Industrial Economy at the Zero Bound

So far, we have made use of a variety of "natural experiments" from recent U.S. experience to try to gauge the potential effectiveness of policy tools at or near the zero bound. In particular, we have analyzed the effects on market expectations of FOMC statements (relevant for strategies that involve the shaping of policy expectations) and considered how the net supply of various Treasury securities influences the yield curve (relevant for strategies that involve the size or composition of the central bank's balance sheet.) The possible effectiveness of such policies in the U.S. context is of great interest, but of course the inferences made are necessarily somewhat indirect, as the policy rate in the United States has remained at least 100 basis points from zero. In contrast, Japan is a modern industrial economy that has actually grappled with the zero lower bound for some seven years now; and although the Japanese economy differs from that of the United States in many ways (notably in its financial structure), its experience still should provide useful lessons for the United States and other industrial countries. In this section we apply some of the same methods used in the U.S. analysis toward understanding the experience of Japan.

An event study of policies of the Bank of Japan

We begin our analysis of Japanese monetary policy by conducting an event study analogous to the one we conducted for the United States. As in the U.S. case, the objective is to analyze how monetary policy expectations at different horizons (as measured in financial markets) respond to central bank statements. Because the Bank of Japan (BOJ) in recent years has used its statements not only to try to shape expectations but also to provide information regarding its programs of quantitative easing and targeted asset purchases, in principle the event study should cast light on the effectiveness of all three types of nonstandard policy options available to an economy at or near the zero bound. In practice, the relatively small number of BOJ policy statements in our sample lead to results that are less sharp than we would like. In the latter part of this section, therefore, we report results based on the estimation of term structure model for Japan.

Two preliminary issues musts be addressed before proceeding to the details of the event study. First, the Bank of Japan (BOJ) did not gain independence until April 1998, which shortens the available sample considerably. (In the period before the BOJ became independent monetary policy in Japan was largely controlled by the Ministry of Finance.) We include in our sample all policy meetings and dates of policy decisions by the BOJ since independence, which gives us 110 observations. Note that, during most of the sample period, the overnight interest rate was very close to zero. Second, we do not have available intraday financial data for Japan, and so we are forced to rely on daily data for our analysis. To complicate matters further, on some occasions BOJ statements have been released just before the close of Japanese financial markets, while at other times they were released just after the close. As we could not easily ascertain the exact timing of all releases, to avoid contamination of the results we examine two-day changes in the financial-market variables considered, from the day before each policy meeting to the day after. The use of a considerably longer event window than in the U.S. analysis increases the scope for factors other than policy actions or announcements to influence the financial variables. The extra noise will reduce the efficiency of our estimates but should not bias the results.

As in the event study for the United States, we employ three market-based measures of policy expectations at various horizons. The first variable is intended to capture the unexpected component of changes in the policy interest rate, the (overnight) call rate. Unfortunately, we cannot measure these surprises in exactly the same way as we do for the FOMC, because there is not an active futures market on the call rate in Japan. Instead, we measure current policy surprises as the change during the event window in the first Euroyen futures contract to expire, which reflects unexpected changes in the policy rate over a slightly longer horizon.[32] Innovations to policy expectations at the one-year and the five-year horizons are measured as changes during the event window in the year-ahead Euroyen futures rate and the five-year zero-coupon Japanese government bond (JGB) yield. The latter two indicators of policy expectations are essentially identical in concept to the analogous rates in our event study for the United States.[33]

As in the U.S. event study, we apply a Cholesky decomposition to derive three candidate factors to explain the movements in the market-based policy indicators in the period around BOJ decisions. By construction, the first factor corresponds to unexpected changes in the current policy setting during the period around BOJ decisions, as measured by the change in the nearest Euroyen futures contract. The second factor, equal to the part of the change in the year-ahead futures contract that is orthogonal to the first factor, is intended to represent in year-ahead policy expectations not explained by

---

[32] These contracts are written on the three-month Euroyen deposit rate at the time of expiration; in practice, the ease with which investors can switch among money-market assets ensures that this rate will be closely tied to the average policy rate expected to prevail over that interval. The Euroyen futures contract expires 1½ months ahead on average, implying that the futures rate corresponds approximately to the expected call rate from 1½ to 4½ months ahead.

[33] The Euroyen futures contracts trade on the Chicago Mercantile Exchange. Data for the zero-coupon five-year JGB yield was taken from Bloomberg.

changes in the current policy setting. Finally, the third factor equals the change in the five-year zero-coupon JGB yield not explained by the first two factors.

The links between these factors and the policy indicators, shown in table 9a, are remarkably similar to those found for the FOMC, as can be seen by comparing table 9a to table 1a in the preceding section. Notably, as in the U.S. event study, we find in the case of Japan that the first factor has an effect on longer-term interest rates that diminishes with maturity, and that the loading of the five-year yield on the second factor is significantly greater than on the first factor.

[Table 9 about here]

However, the magnitudes of the three factors, shown in table 9b, differ from the U.S. case. In particular, the first and second factors are much smaller (as measured by their standard deviations, the diagonal elements in the table) than in the U.S. event study (compare to table 1b). That is, changes in both current and year-ahead policy expectations in periods around BOJ decisions have been more subdued than in the U.S. case. However, the standard deviation of the third factor, which reflects longer-horizon policy expectations, is about the same, at 3.5 basis points, in the Japanese and U.S. cases. The influence of the zero bound may explain the limited variation in the first two factors; both current and year-ahead futures rates were near zero over much of the sample, which restricted changes in policy expectations and rates in the downward direction at least. However, the zero bound is not the whole story; even in the period before 2001, when the year-ahead futures rate was generally above 50 basis points, the standard deviation of the second factor was only slightly higher (3.9 basis points) than in the sample as a whole.

Table 9. Japan: Decomposition of policy indicators into factors

a.   Loadings of market-based policy indicators on candidate factors

Effect of factor on:	First factor	Second factor	Third factor
Current policy setting	1.00	0.00	0.00
Year-ahead futures rate	0.55	1.00	0.00
Five-year yield	0.32	0.64	1.00

b. Contributions of factors to the standard deviations of policy indicators

Standard deviation of the effect of factor on:	First factor	Second factor	Third factor
Current policy setting	3.4	0	0
Year-ahead futures rate	1.9	3.0	0
Five-year yield	1.1	1.9	3.5

Note: Standard deviations are measured in basis points
The sample period is April 1998 through the present.

Overall, it appears that the scope for the Bank of Japan to "use" the second factor, or its willingness to do, was less than in the case of the Federal Reserve over the same period.[34]

As in the U.S. event study, we are interested in examining the relationship between the three factors describing changes in policy expectations and the statements issued by the central bank. We again define a dummy variable, STATEMENT, that equals one on dates in which the BOJ released policy statements and zero otherwise. As in the U.S. analysis, we also define a dummy variable, STATEMENT SURPRISE, that indicates statements that were deemed to be surprising in significant aspects to market participants. To determine which statements were "surprises" we again relied on several after-the-fact documents, including internal write-ups prepared by the staff of the Federal Reserve Bank of New York and stories in the Wall Street Journal, and one before-the-fact source, a series of commentaries prepared by Nikko/Citigroup just before each BOJ meeting.

Of the 110 observations in our sample, 19 involved the release of statements about the economy or monetary policy; we exclude ten statements concerned only with various technical aspects of monetary policy operations without implications for the economic or policy outlook. Of these 19 statements, 10 were identified by our methods as "surprises." The Appendix describes all statements over the period and shows how we coded them [to be provided].

As in the U.S. event study, we proceeded by regressing the squared factors on the dummy variables indicating statements and surprising statements. Again, following Kohn and Sack (2003), the use of the squared factors as dependent variables allows us to

---

[34] An institutional explanation for the smaller second factor in Japan is the BOJ's practice of releasing policy statements only in conjunction with policy actions, rather than after every scheduled meeting.

determine whether statements were associated with large changes in policy expectations (large realizations of the factors), without requiring us to specify the "direction" of the statements.

The regression results, shown in table 10, differ considerably from those found for the Federal Reserve (compare table 2). First, we find that the square of the first factor has a statistically significant relationship to STATEMENT SURPRISE but not to STATEMENT. This suggests that, unlike the FOMC, which appears reluctant to surprise in terms of both the policy setting and the statement at the same meeting, the BOJ often did so. Indeed, a review of the record shows that the BOJ on several occasions combined announcements of major policy innovations with unexpected changes in the setting of the interest rate. Notably, the announcement of the adoption of the zero interest rate policy (ZIRP) on February 12, 1999, coincided with a 9- basis-point policy-rate surprise under our measure, as the call rate was reduced from 25 basis points to a value "as low as possible," initially 15 basis points; and the introduction of quantitative easing on March 19, 2001, coincided with an 11-basis-point policy surprise, as the call rate was reduced from 12.5 basis points to essentially zero.

[Table 10 about here]

Second, and in striking contrast with the results for the FOMC, we find no evident relationship between the second factor and the release of statements, whether surprising or not. This result, together with the small magnitude of the second factor already reported, suggests again that the BOJ was either unable or unwilling to influence year-ahead policy expectations with its statements. (In making this interpretation, however, we should also keep in mind that the Japanese sample is much smaller.)

Table 10.   Japan: Regressions of Squared Factors on Statement Dummy Variables

Independent variable	Dependent variable		
	First factor	Second factor	Third factor
Constant	7.4	8.2	**10.9**
	(1.79)	(2.78)	(4.18)
Statement	-1.2	-1.2	-5.7
	(-0.09)	(-0.12)	(-0.66)
Statement Surprise	**50.5**	10.4	**25.8**
	(2.79)	(0.81)	(2.25)
Adj. R-Squared	0.12	0.01	0.06

t-statistics are given in parentheses. Coefficients in bold are significant at the 5 percent level.

Third, in Japan, unlike the U.S., the size of the third factor is linked to the issuance of surprising statements by the central bank. However, this finding is largely the product of a single observation, the February 12, 1999 statement announcing the introduction of the ZIRP. Standard reasoning suggests that the announcement of the ZIRP should have influenced the third factor by leading to a drop in long-term bond yields; surprisingly, the third factor actually rose by 14 basis points that day. Our reading suggests that market participants were disappointed that the statement did not announce large-scale BOJ purchases of JGBs, as had been rumored. Perhaps then we should think of this important observation as consisting of two surprises working in opposite directions.

To examine the effects of BOJ statements further, we categorized the surprising statements into three categories: (1) statements providing new information about the likely path of policy (PATH SURPRISE), in analogy to the event study for the Federal Reserve; (2) statements announcing an unexpected change in the BOJ's target for purchases of JGBs (JGB surprise); and (3) statements announcing unexpected changes in the BOJ's target for current account balances, in the period following the introduction of quantitative easing (CAB SURPRISE). In principle, this categorization should provide information on the relative effects of changes in policy expectations, targeted purchases of securities, and quantitative easing. Note that statements were allowed to fall into more than one category, if appropriate.

Again, the problems arising from a small sample are apparent, as the number of statements in each category is relatively small. We identified only two statements as potential "path surprises": the introductions of the ZIRP in February 1999 and of quantitative easing in March 2001. These, of course, represented major shifts in policy strategy, and thus their effects may differ from the policy path surprises identified in the U.S. event study. Five BOJ statements announced changes in the target for JGB purchases (including the implementation of the quantitative easing program), three of which we identified as surprises to the market. Ten statements during the sample period announced changes in the target for CABs (including the statement that initiated the program), of which six were identified as surprises to the market.

Because the direction as well as magnitude of statement effects is important, we report here results based on the "signed" dummy variable approach introduced in the previous section.[35] Specifically, for each dummy variable corresponding to a surprising statement, we assigned a value of 1 for statements that would be expected to increase interest rates and a value of -1 for statements that would be expected to lower interest rates. Non-surprising statements were coded as zeros. We then regressed the levels of each of the three factors on the signed dummy variables, allowing us to judge not only whether statements influenced expectations but whether expectations were influenced in the expected direction.

We added one further innovation to the analysis at this point. Our focus thus far has been on the link at various horizons between central bank policy actions and statements on the one hand and interest rates on the other. However, the logic of quantitative easing and targeted asset purchases implies that the most important effects of these policies may be felt on the prices of assets other than government bonds. To check this possibility, we included a fourth candidate factor in this event study, defined as the

---

[35] We also tried regressing the squared values of the factors on the various dummies; this exercise did not add much information to that already reported in Table 11.

73

portion of the change in the Nikkei 500 stock index during the event window that is orthogonal to the other three factors. That is, the fourth factor reflects the impact of the BOJ's action and statement on Japanese equity values (an important alternative class of asset), holding constant market expectations about current and future interest rates.[36] If BOJ policy decisions are influencing asset prices other than through expectational channels, this factor should pick that up.

The results, shown in table 11, amplify but also generally confirm the results discussed earlier in the section. We saw earlier that surprises in the policy setting (the first factor) and in the statement tend to be associated in Japan. Table 11 (column 1) shows that these surprises tend to be in the same direction (that is, both toward tightening or both toward ease), consistent with the earlier discussion. Further (column 2), unanticipated changes in the policy setting also seemed to be associated with statements that provide information on the future path of policy (that is, the PATH SURPRISE dummy accounts for the entire relationship between the first factor and statement surprises). This result is driven primarily by the announcements of the ZIRP and the quantitative easing program, which (as already mentioned) were associated with surprises in the policy setting as well.

We continue to find no significant relationship between the second factor (the innovation in year-ahead policy expectations) and BOJ statements, even with this finer categorization of statements (columns 3 and 4 of the table). This result is the strongest and most important contrast between the findings for the BOJ and for the Federal Reserve.

---

[36] It turns out that 99.2 percent of the variance of stock prices during the event window is orthogonal to the first three factors, that is, almost all of the change in stock prices is explained by the fourth factor, unrelated to interest rates.

The level of the third factor (which, recall, corresponds to the fluctuation in the yield on JGBs during the event window that is not explained by current or year-ahead policy expectations) appears to be linked with certain types of statements. As the column 6 in the table shows, a statement that surprises the market in suggesting that policy will be tighter in the future (that is, a positive path surprise) causes five-year yields to fall; the effect is statistically significant. This finding can be rationalized by the argument that a near-term tightening lowers inflation expectations and thus nominal rates at long horizons. Perhaps more interesting, the third factor also has a statistically significant link to JGB surprises; that is, BOJ statements announcing unexpectedly large targets for JGB purchases (an easing move, so coded as -1) are associated with decline in the yield on five-year JGBs, as should be the case if targeted bond purchases by the central bank affect their yields. However, the estimated effect, though statistically significant, is not large (5 basis points), and is of necessity based on relatively few observations.

[Table 11 about here]

The results for the fourth factor, which is essentially the change in the stock market during the event window, are of interest. Table 11 (columns 7-8) shows that the stock market drops between 1 and 2 percent on average when the BOJ issues a surprisingly hawkish statement. The statistically strongest link is to BOJ announcements of new CAB targets. Inspection of the data shows that on three of the six occasions on which the BOJ made surprise announcements of increases in its target for current account balances, the Nikkei 500 rose between 3 and 6 percent, including a 5.9 percent increase on the announcement of the quantitative easing policy. On one other such occasion the market rose nearly 2 percent. Thus, in the event study at least, quantitative easing

Table 11. Japan: Regressions of Factors (in Levels) on Signed Statement Dummy Variables

	Factor 1		Factor 2		Factor 3		Factor 4	
	(1)	(2)	(3)	(4)	(5)	(6)	(7)	(8)
Signed Statement Surprise	**4.75** (4.80)	--	1.1 (1.14)	--	0.5 (1.11)	--	-1.12 (-1.90)	
Signed Path Surprise	--	**9.8** (4.13)	--	-2.2 (-1.01)	--	**-6.3** (-2.54)		-1.94 (-1.45)
Signed JGB Surprise	--	0.9 (0.53)	--	-2.7 (-1.64)	--	**5.1** (2.80)		-1.16 (-1.17)
Signed CAB Surprise	--	0.4 (0.26)	--	0.4 (0.28)	--	-0.0 (-0.02)		**-1.70** (-2.0)
Adj. R-Squared	0.17	0.16	0.01	0.03	0.06	0.13	0.02	0.10

t-statistics are in parentheses. Coefficients in bold are significant at the 5 percent level.

appears to provide a positive impetus to the stock market, with both current and future interest-rate expectations held constant.

Overall, two general conclusions emerge from the BOJ event study. First, there is little evidence that the BOJ used its statements to influence near-term policy expectations during this period. This contradicts the finding of other research that the ZIRP was effective; we revisit this issue below. Second, there is some tentative support here for the view that asset prices respond to quantitative easing and targeted asset purchases; specifically, we find statistically significant links between JGB purchases and JGB yields on the one hand, and between quantitative easing and stock prices on the other. Whether these latter effects were large enough to have a significant influence on the Japanese economy will be addressed next.

A benchmark term-structure model for Japan

As a final exercise, we estimate a benchmark term-structure model for Japan and compare the results to actual term-structure behavior. As in the U.S. case, the model is a no-arbitrage affine term structure model driven by observable factors. The underlying factors are assumed be the unemployment rate, the inflation rate (12-month change in the CPI), the overnight call rate, and the year-ahead Euroyen futures rate. (These variables are closely analogous to those used for the U.S. estimation, except that we do not have a monthly inflation expectation measure to include.) The dynamics of the factors are determined by an estimated VAR with four lags, where the VAR is estimated using monthly data over the sample period June 1982 to May 2004.[37]

---

[37] Data on the Euroyen futures rate is available only from June 1989; for dates prior to June 1989 we used a proxy, constructed by regressing the futures rate on the 5-year JGB yield and the call rate for the sample period June 1989 – May 1999, then using fitted values of the Euroyen futures rate as the proxy.

With the estimated VAR in hand, we then fit the no-arbitrage term structure model using data from the JGB market. The data on JGB yields are month-average zero-coupon yields at maturities of six months and one, two, three, five, seven, and ten years, obtained from Bloomberg for the period back to April 1989. The prices of risk are estimated using yield curve data from April 1989 to December 1997, based on the VAR dynamics estimated over the full sample. The fit of the model is quite good (as can be seen in figure 10). We show the fit of the model through 1997 only; as we discuss momentarily, for the period after 1997 we need to make an adjustment for the proximity of short-term yields to the ZLB.

When short-term interest rates fall to very low levels, the zero bound constraint begins to influence the shape of the yield curve. One effect is that the zero bound reduces the possibility of declines in interest rates (and obviously eliminates them at short-term maturities), which limits the scope for capital gains on fixed-income securities. To compensate for this, investors will demand higher yields on fixed-income assets (as described in Bomfim (2003), thereby steepening the yield curve (see also Ruge-Murcia, 2002).

We can account for this effect in our VAR model. The price of a two-year note, for example, should equal the expected product of the pricing kernel over the next 24 months:

(9) $$P_t^{24} = E_t \left[m_{t+1} m_{t+2} m_{t+3} ... m_{t+24} \right].$$

We computed the bond price defined by (9) by performing 10,000 simulations of the model over the subsequent 24 months, determining the path of the pricing kernel in each iteration, and then taking the average of the product of the pricing kernel over all simulations. This exercise can be performed both ignoring the zero bound and imposing the zero bound.

If we perform the simulations without imposing the zero bound, the predicted bond prices will (asymptotically) be the same as those obtained directly from the VAR (such as those shown in figure 10), since the VAR dynamics do not recognize the presence of the zero bound constraint. To impose the zero bound, in each simulation we assume that in any month that the policy rate would go negative, there is a shock to the policy rate sufficient to pull it back to zero.[38] We can rigorously price fixed income assets according to (9) under these alternative simulations, which then allows us to estimate the effects of the zero bound on the term structure. In this exercise, we account for the fact that investors, in valuing bonds, take into account the effect of the zero bound on the future path of short-term interest rates, as well as its effects on all of the state variables that affect the prices of risk.[39]

Figure 11 shows the results from this exercise for four representative months—December 1998 (several months before the introduction of the ZIRP), May 1999 (several months after the ZIRP), November 2000 (several months after the end of the ZIRP but before the introduction of the QEP) and June 2001 (several months after the introduction of QEP). The influence of the zero bound (shown by the shift in the predicted yield curve from the thin solid line to the thick solid line) shifts up the yield curve in all cases, where the magnitude of the shift depends on the proximity of rates to the bound. More

---

[38] The year-ahead futures rate is assumed to respond endogenously to these policy shocks, based on a Cholesky decomposition in which the policy rate is ordered second-to-last and the futures rate is ordered last. Without this endogenous response, the futures rate would often go negative.

[39] This exercise seems to get us a long way towards properly accounting for the effects of the zero bound on the term structure of interest rates, but it still has some shortcomings. Specifically, the dynamics of the VAR and the relationship between risk prices and economic variables may change in important ways near the zero bound, so that their dynamics are not well captured by the VAR with policy shocks. A similar criticism applies to other work on the effects of the zero bound, such as that of Bomfim [date].

importantly, the predicted yield curves (considering the zero bound) tend to lie above the actual yield curves. In other words, the VAR term structure model has difficulty explaining the low levels of JGB yields during this period.

This result holds even though the VAR has a very pessimistic view of the economy over this period. For most of the period since 1998, the VAR predicts that deflation will persist for some time and short-term interest rates will remain very low. This forecast, however, probably should be regarded with some skepticism. The VAR is estimated over a sample in which unemployment was rising and inflation falling; as a result, it finds that these variables are very persistent and extrapolates these trends. One could presumably improve upon that forecast by taking into consideration additional information or a more detailed model. Nevertheless, the interesting finding for our purposes is that, even given the VAR's downbeat projections of for short-term interest rates, actual longer-term JGB yields seem to have been lower than projected by the model.

An interesting question, then, is whether the low level of JGB yields was associated with the policies of the Bank of Japan. Figure 11 suggests that the ZIRP and the QEP may have played some role. As can be seen, the deviation between the predicted and actual yields widened after the introduction of the ZIRP, narrowed once the policy was abandoned, and widened again after the introduction of the QEP. Put differently, the JGB yield curve shifted down noticeably in the months surrounding the announcement of these two policies. By contrast, the yield curves predicted by the model did not shift down much, in large part because the scope for a fall in JGB yields was limited by the zero bound. As we have noted earlier, assessing the effects of the ZIRP and especially the QEP are in general difficult because of the problems of controlling for other factors influencing yields over the periods of these policies. It is intriguing, at least, that when we control (at least roughly) for macroeconomic conditions and the current stance of monetary policy, as well as for the effects on longer-term rates of the "option" created by the presence of the zero bound, we still find that the Japanese term structure is lower than predicted. Moreover, the deviation of the actual term structure and the predicted pattern of yields increased immediately following the introductions of ZIRP and QEP. This evidence, moreso than the event study analysis described above, gives some reason to believe that non-standard policies in Japan have been effective at lowering longer-term interest rates. Whether the lower rates led to a material strengthening of the economy is beyond the scope of our discussion here.

[Figure 10 about here]

[Figure 11 about here]

Conclusion

In brief, we have developed new empirical evidence on the likely effects of non-standard monetary policies near the zero bound. Notably, the Federal Reserve has successfully used its communications to affect expectations of future policies and thus longer-term yields. We also find some evidence that relative supplies of securities matter for yields in the United States, a necessary condition for achieving the desired effects from targeted asset purchases. The event studies for Japan do not provide much evidence that the Bank of Japan has been successful in using nonstandard policies, but the term structure analysis does suggest that longer-term yields have been lower than might have

Figure 10. Actual and Predicted JGB Yields
Percent

Two-year JGB Yield

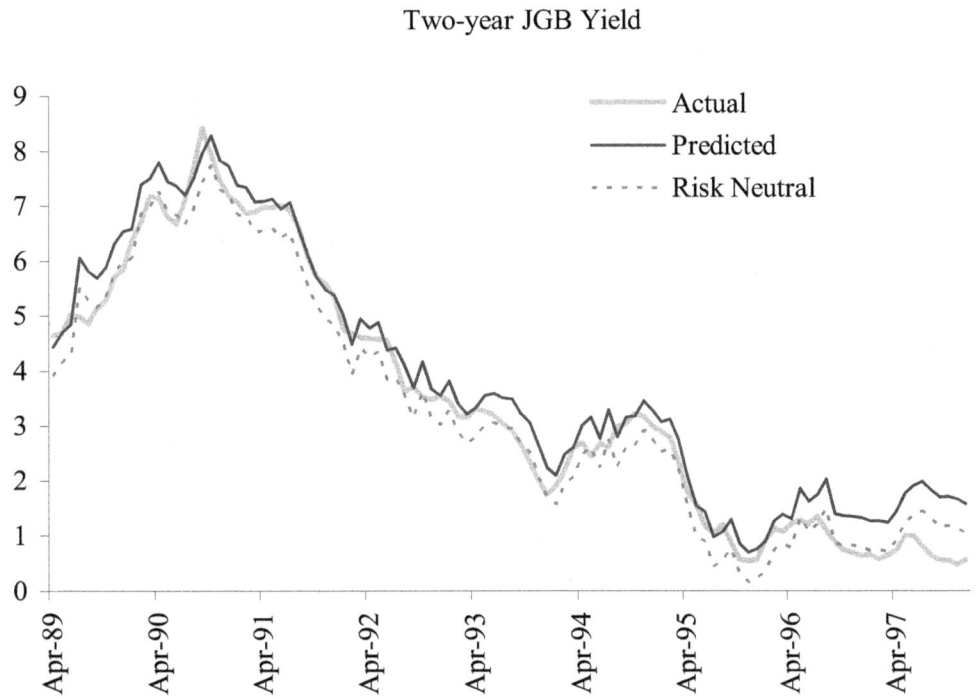

Ten-year JGB Yield

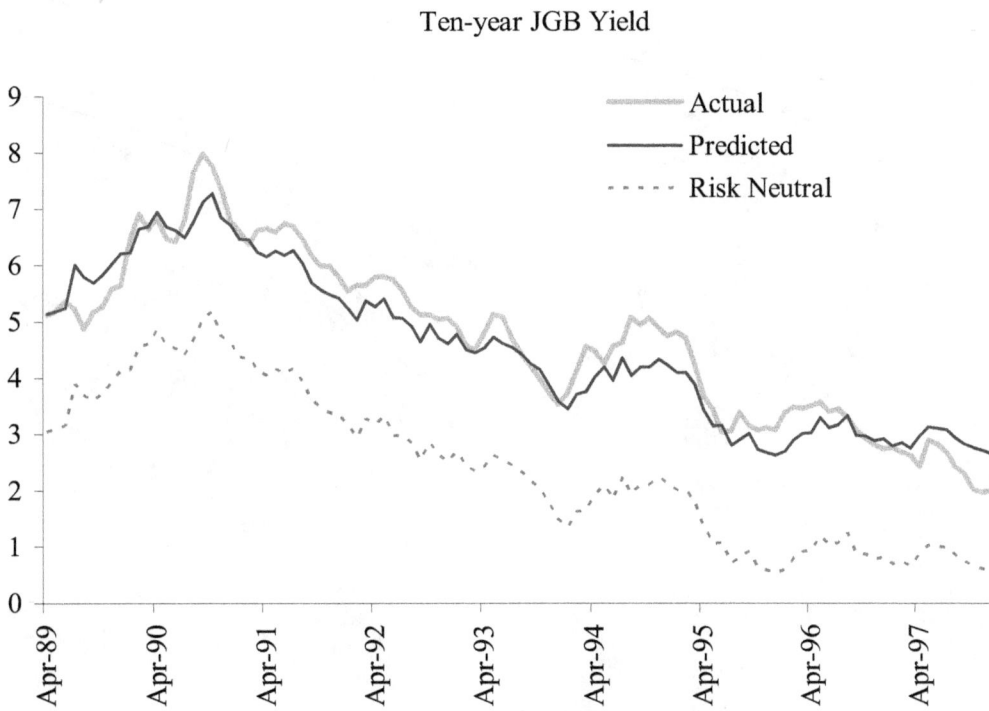

Figure 11. JGB Yield Curve around Bank of Japan Policy Announcements

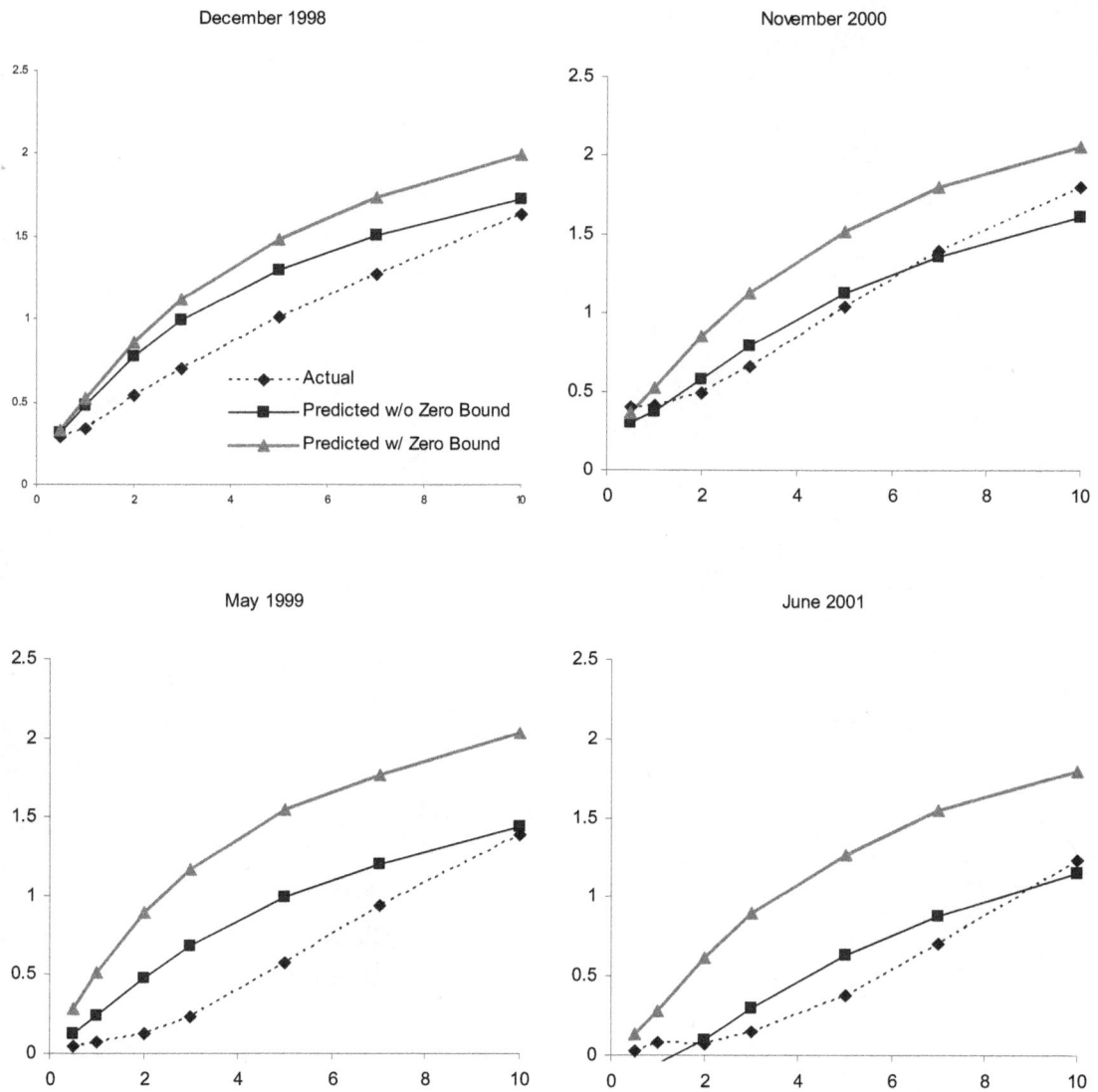

December 1998

November 2000

May 1999

June 2001

been expected in recent years, holding open the possibility that the ZIRP and quantitative easing policies have had beneficial effects.

Despite our evidence that alternative policy measures have some effect, we remain cautious about relying on such approaches. We believe that our findings go some way to refuting the strong hypothesis that nonstandard policy actions, including quantitative easing and targeted asset purchases, cannot be successful in a modern industrial economy. However, the effects of such policies remain quantitatively quite uncertain. Thus we believe that policymakers should continue to maintain an inflation buffer and to act preemptively against emerging deflationary risks (Reifschneider and Williams, 2000). There are tradeoffs, of course, in that erring toward the side of ease when rates are low tends to create an inflation bias; but the goal of zero inflation seems unwise in any case, and a systematic tendency to err toward an easier policy when adverse shocks bulk large and nominal interest rates are low can be offset by a willingness to unwind that accommodation quickly once the situation clears.

Shaping investor expectations through communication does appear to be a viable strategy, as suggested by Eggertsson and Woodford (2003a,b). By persuading the public that the policy rate will remain low for a longer period than expected, central bankers can reduce long-term rates and provide some impetus to the economy, even if the short-term rate is close to zero. However, for credibility to be maintained, the central bank's commitments must be consistent with the public's understanding of the policymakers' objectives and outlook for the economy.

References

Adam, Klaus and Roberto Billi. 2004. "Optimal Monetary Policy under Commitment with a Zero Bound on Nominal Interest Rates," Working Paper, European Central Bank.

Ahearne, Alan, Joseph Gagnon, Jane Haltmaier and Steve Kamin, et al. 2002. "Preventing Deflation: Lessons from Japan's Experience in the 1990s," Board of Governors of the Federal Reserve System, International Finance Discussion Paper 729.

Akerlof, George, William Dickens, and George Perry. 1996. "The Macroeconomics of Low Inflation." *Brookings Papers on Economic Activity*, (1): 1-76.

Andres, Javier, J. David Lopez-Salido, and Edward Nelson. 2003. "Tobin's Imperfect Asset Substitution in Optimizing General Equilibrium." Presented at the James Tobin Symposium, sponsored by the *Journal of Money, Credit, and Banking* and the Federal Reserve Bank of Chicago, November 14-15.

Ang, Andrew, and Monika Piazzesi. 2003. "A No-Arbitrage Vector Autoregression of Term Structure Dynamics with Macroeconomic and Latent Variables." *Journal of Monetary Economics*, 50: 745-87.

Ang, Andrew, Monika Piazzesi, and Min Wei. 2003. "What Does the Yield Curve Tell Us About GDP Growth?" Columbia University and University of Chicago, Working Paper, October.

Auerbach, Alan and William Gale. 2000. "Perspectives on the Budget Surplus." *National Tax Journal*, 53: 459-72.

Auerbach, Alan, and Maurice Obstfeld. 2004. "The Case for Open Market Purchases in a Liquidity Trap." Working paper, University of California at Berkeley.

Baba, Naohiko, Shinichi Nishioka, Nobuyuki Oda, Maasaki Shirakawa, Kazuo Ueda, and Hiroshi Ugai. 2004. "Japan's Deflation, Problems in the Financial System, and Monetary Policy." Presented at BIS conference, "Understanding Low Inflation and Deflation," June 19, Brunnen, Switzerland.

Benhabib, Jess, Stephanie Schmitt-Grohe, and Martin Uribe. 2002. "Avoiding Liquidity Traps." *Journal of Political Economy*, 110(3): 535-63.

Bernanke, Ben. 2002. "Deflation: Making Sure 'It' Doesn't Happen Here." Remarks before the National Economists' Club, Washington D.C., November 21. http://www.federalreserve.gov/boarddocs/speeches/2002/20021121/default.htm

Bernanke, Ben. 2003. "Some Thoughts on Monetary Policy in Japan." Speech to the Japan Society of Monetary Economics, Tokyo, May 31. http://www.federalreserve.gov/boarddocs/speeches/2003/20030531/default.htm

Bernanke, Ben, and Kenneth Kuttner. 2004. "Why Does Monetary Policy Affect the Stock Market?" *Journal of Finance*, forthcoming.

Bernanke, Ben, and Vincent Reinhart. 2004. "Conducting Monetary Policy at Very Low Short-Term Interest Rates," *American Economic Review*, 94(2): 85-90.

Blinder, Alan. 2000. "Monetary Policy at the Zero Lower Bound: Balancing the Risks: Summary Panel." *Journal of Money, Credit and Banking*, 32 (4):1093-99.

Bolder, David J. 2001. "Affine Term-Structure Models: Theory and Implementation." Working Paper 2001-15. Ottawa: Bank of Canada.

Bomfim, Antulio. 2003. "Interest Rates as Options: Assessing the Markets' View of the Liquidity Trap." Working Paper, Board of Governors of the Federal Reserve System, July.

Brainard, William, and James Tobin. 1968. "Pitfalls in Financial Model-Building," *American Economic Review*, 58(2), May: 99-123.

Clouse, James, Dale Henderson, Athanasios Orphanides, David Small, and Peter Tinsley. 2003. "Monetary Policy when the Nominal Short-Term Interest Rate Is Zero." Berkeley Electronic Press, *Topics in Macroeconomics*, 3(1), Article 12. http://www.bepress.com/bejm/topics/vol3/iss1/art12.

Coenen, Günter, Athanasios Orphanides, and VolkerWieland. 2004. "Price Stability and Monetary Policy Effectiveness when Nominal Interest Rates are Bounded at Zero." Berkeley Electronic Press, *Advances in Macroeconomics*, 4 (1), Article 1. http://www.bepress.com/bejm/advances/vol4/iss1/art1.

Cox, J. C., Ingersoll, J. E., and Ross, S. A. 1985. "A Theory of the Term Structure of Interest Rates." *Econometrica*, 53(2): 385-407.

Duffie, Darrell, and Rui Kan. 1996. "A Yield-Factor Model of Interest Rates." *Mathematical Finance*, 6(4): 379-406.

Eichengreen, Barry, and Peter Garber. 1991. "Before the Accord: U.S. Monetary-Financial Policy, 1945-51." In G. Hubbard, ed., *Financial Markets and Financial Crisis*. Chicago: University of Chicago Press.

Eggertsson, Gauti, and Michael Woodford. 2003a. "The Zero Bound on Interest Rates and Optimal Monetary Policy." *Brookings Papers on Economic Activity*, 1: 139-233.

Eggertsson, Gauti, and Michael Woodford. 2003b. "Optimal Monetary Policy in a Liquidity Trap." NBER Working Paper 9968.

Feldstein, Martin. 1997. "The Costs and Benefits of Going from Low Inflation to Price Stability." In Christina Romer and David Romer, eds., *Reducing Inflation: Motivation and Strategy*. Chicago: University of Chicago Press.

Fischer, Stanley. 1996. "Why Are Central Banks Pursuing Long-Run Price Stability?" In *Achieving Price Stability*, Kansas City: Federal Reserve Bank of Kansas City.

Fisher, M., D. Nychka, and D. Zervos. 1995. "Fitting the Term Structure of Interest Rates with Smoothing Splines." Board of Governors of the Federal Reserve System, Finance and Economics Discussion Paper 95-1.

Friedman, Benjamin, and Kenneth Kuttner. 1998. "Indicator Properties of the Paper-Bill Spread: Lessons from Recent Experience." *Review of Economics & Statistics*, 80 (February): 34-44.

Friedman, Milton. 1969. *The Optimum Quantity of Money and Other Essays*. Chicago: Aldine.

Fujiki, Hiroshi and Shigenori Shiratsuka. 2002. "Policy Duration Effect under the Zero Interest Rate Policy in 1999-2000: Evidence from Japan's Money Market Data." *Monetary and Economic Studies*, January, 20(1): 1-31.

Gürkaynak, Refet, Brian Sack, and Eric Swanson. 2004. "Measuring the Response of Asset Prices to Monetary Policy Actions and Statements," Board of Governors of the Federal Reserve System, working paper, July.

Holland, Thomas. 1969. "'Operation Twist' and the Movement of Interest Rates and Related Economic Time Series." *International Economic Review*, 10(3): 260-5.

Hutchinson, William, and Mark Toma. 1991. "The Bond Price Support Program as a Change in Policy Regimes: Evidence from the Term Structure of Interest Rates." *Journal of Money, Credit, and Banking*, 23(3): 367-82.

Kimura, Takeshi, Hiroshi Kobayashi, Jun Muranaga, and Hiroshi Ugai. 2002. "The Effect of 'Quantitative Monetary Easing' at Zero Interest Rates." IMES Discussion Paper Series, 2002-E-22. Tokyo: Bank of Japan.

Kohn, Donald, and Brian Sack. 2003. "Central Bank Talk: Does It Matter and Why?" Board of Governors of the Federal Reserve System, Finance and Economics Discussion Series, 2003-55.

Krugman, Paul. 1998. "It's Baaack! Japan's Slump and the Return of the Liquidity Trap." *Brookings Papers on Economic Activity* 2: 137-87.

Kuttner, Kenneth. 2001. "Monetary Policy Surprises and Interest Rates: Evidence from Fed Funds Futures." *Journal of Monetary Economics*, 47(3): 523-44.

Longstaff, F.A., and E. S. Schwartz. 1992. "A Two-Factor Interest Rate Model and Contingent Claims Evaluation." *The Journal of Fixed Income*, 2(3): 16-23.

Marumo, Kohei, Takashi Nakayama, Shinichi Nishioka, and Toshihiro Yoshida. 2003. "Extracting Market Expectations on the Duration of the Zero Interest Rate Policy from Japan's Bond Prices." Financial Markets Department Working Paper 03-E-2. Tokyo: Bank of Japan.

Meltzer, Allan. 1999. "Comments: What More Can the Bank of Japan Do?" Bank of Japan, *Monetary and Economic Studies*, 17, December: 189-191.

Meltzer, Allan. 2001. "Monetary Transmission at Low Inflation: Some Clues from Japan." Bank of Japan, *Monetary and Economic Studies* 19 (S-1), February: 13-34.

Modigliani, Franco, and Richard Sutch. 1966. "Innovations in Interest Rate Policy." *American Economic Review*, 52(1/2): 178-97.

Modigliani, Franco, and Richard Sutch. 1967. "Debt Management and the Term Structure of Interest Rates: An Empirical Analysis of Recent Experience." *Journal of Political Economy* 75(4, part 2): 569-89.

Nagayasu, Jun. 2004. "The Term Structure of Interest Rates and Monetary Policy During a Zero Interest Rate Period." Bank of Japan, Monetary and Economic Studies, 22(2), May: 19-43.

Okina, Kunio, and Shigenori Shiratsuka. 2004. "Policy Commitment and Expectation Formation: Japan's Experience under Zero Interest Rates." *North American Journal of Economics and Finance*, 15 (1): 75-100.

Phelps, Edmund. 1972. *Inflation Policy and Unemployment Theory*. London: Macmillan.

Reifschneider, David, and John Williams. 2000. "Three Lessons for Monetary Policy in a Low-Inflation Era." *Journal of Money, Credit, and Banking*, 32: 936-966.

Reinhart, Vincent, and Brian Sack. 2000. "The Economic Consequences of Disappearing Government Debt." *Brookings Papers on Economic Activity*, 2: 163-220.

Roley, V. Vance. 1982. "The Effect of Federal Debt-Management Policy on Corporate Bond and Equity Yields." *Quarterly Journal of Economics*, 97(4): 645-68.

Romer, Christina. 1992. "What Ended the Great Depression?" *Journal of Economic History*, 52(4): 757-84.

Rudebusch, Glenn, and Tao Wu. 2003. "A Macro-Finance Model of the Term Structure, Monetary Policy, and the Economy," Federal Reserve Bank of San Francisco, working paper 2003-17, September.

Ruge-Murcia, Franciso. 2002. "Some Implications of the Zero Lower Bound on Interest Rates for the Term Structure and Monetary Policy." Cahier 06-2002. Montreal: Université de Montreal.

Shirakawa, Masaaki. 2002. "One Year Under 'Quantitative Easing'." Bank of Japan, IMES Discussion Paper No. 2002-E-3.

Summers, Lawrence. 1991. "Panel Discussion: How Should Long-Term Monetary Policy Be Determined?" *Journal of Money, Credit, and Banking* 23(3, Part 2): 625-31.

Svensson, Lars. 2001. "The Zero Bound in an Open Economy: A Foolproof Way of Escaping from a Liquidity Trap." Bank of Japan, Monetary and Economic Studies, 19(S-1), February: 277-312.

Svensson, Lars. 2003. "Escaping from a Liquidity Trap and Deflation: the Foolproof Way and Others." *Journal of Economic Perspectives*, 17(4), Fall: 145-166.

Takeda, Y., and Y. Yajima. 2002. "How the Japanese Government Bond Market Has Responded to the Zero Interest Rate Policy." NLI Research.

Temin, Peter and Barrie Wigmore. 1990. "The End of One Big Deflation." *Explorations in Economic History*, 27 (October): 483-502.

Tobin, James. 1969. "A General Equilibrium Approach to Monetary Theory." *Journal of Money, Credit, and Banking*, 1(1), February: 15-29.

Tobin, James. 1974. *The New Economics: One Decade Older*. Princeton, NJ: Princeton University Press.

Toma, Mark. 1992. "Interest Rate Controls: The United States in the 1940s." *Journal of Economic History*, 52(3): 631-50.

Vasicek, O.A. 1977. "An Equilibrium Characterization of the Term Structure." *Journal of Financial Economics*, 5: 177-88.

Woodford, Michael. 2003. *Money, Interest, and Prices*. Princeton, NJ: Princeton University Press.

www.ingramcontent.com/pod-product-compliance
Lightning Source LLC
Chambersburg PA
CBHW080849300326
41935CB00040B/1692